'Flush with creative ideas and expert guidance, this book is an excellent resource for any helping professional working with adolescents in a group context. The dialectical view is innovative and specifically adaptive to engaging, therapeutic, and fun work with adolescents. I would want to both lead a group using this approach and be a group member.'

Professor Matt Englar-Carlson, *Department of Counseling, California State University, Fullerton, co-author of* Learning Group Leadership: An Experiential Approach *(2014, Sage Publications)*

'Mortola & Gans draw on their vast experience of group leadership to guide clinicians through the delicate art of creating developmentally and relationally attuned group spaces. Groupwork is so powerful for young people and this compelling and practical guide demonstrates why. A must-read for group leaders with this age group.'

Bronagh Starrs, *Programme Director of Adolescent Psychotherapy, Dublin Counselling and Therapy Centre, Dublin, Ireland*

'This is a unique counseling group curriculum which provides a dialectical framework and guided sessions based on the authors' shared experience leading hundreds of counseling groups with adolescents. I wholeheartedly recommend it to teach social and emotional skills in schools and professional settings, deepening a teen's sense of belonging and sense of self.'

Laura Barbour, PhD, LPSC, *Lewis & Clark Graduate School of Education and Counseling; Past President of the Oregon School Counselor Association*

Strengthening Social Connections and Individual Resilience in Adolescence

This book introduces a group counseling curriculum that provides both a foundation to confidently lead a counseling group for adolescents and inspiration for how a group leader can adapt and modify the text in a range of settings.

The curriculum is three-fold, corresponding with the three major sections of the text. In Part One of the text, the authors provide a conceptual and practical way of understanding two matters: first, the critical leadership challenges faced by group counselors as well as the skills they need to navigate those challenges successfully, and second, the critical developmental challenges faced by adolescents and the skills they need to navigate those challenges successfully. Part Two introduces a nine-week social skills curriculum – *Belong and Be You* – designed and modified over ten years of use to help adolescents be better socially connected as well as confidently independent. Part Three provides an additional resource which is meant to be used in tandem with the curriculum: 40 strategic stories on four different themes contributed by faculty and students.

This book will benefit school counselors and group counselors working with adolescents to successfully navigate group leadership and help students embrace themselves and find belonging.

Peter Mortola, PhD, is a Professor of Counseling, Therapy and School Psychology at Lewis & Clark College's Graduate School of Education and Counseling in Portland, Oregon.

Diane Gans, MA, LPC, is a psychotherapist and educator who has served children and their families for over 25 years as both a classroom teacher and counselor in private practice.

Strengthening Social Connections and Individual Resilience in Adolescence

The *Belong and Be You* Curriculum

Peter Mortola and Diane Gans

Routledge
Taylor & Francis Group

NEW YORK AND LONDON

Cover image by Peter Mortola

First published 2024
by Routledge
605 Third Avenue, New York, NY 10158

and by Routledge
4 Park Square, Milton Park, Abingdon, Oxon, OX14 4RN

Routledge is an imprint of the Taylor & Francis Group, an informa business

Library of Congress Cataloging-in-Publication Data
Names: Mortola, Peter, author. | Gans, Diane, author.
Title: Strengthening social connections and individual resilience
in adolescence: the belong and be you curriculum/Peter
Mortola, PhD and Diane Gans, MA.
Description: Abingdon, Oxon; New York, NY: Routledge, 2024. |
Includes bibliographical references and index. |
Identifiers: LCCN 2023021545 (print) |
LCCN 2023021546 (ebook) | ISBN 9781032437682 (hardback) |
ISBN 9781032437675 (paperback) | ISBN 9781003368779 (ebook)
Subjects: LCSH: Social skills in adolescence. | Social interaction
in adolescence. | Resilience (Personality trait) in adolescence. |
Group counseling for teenagers.
Classification: LCC HQ796 .M625 2024 (print) |
LCC HQ796 (ebook) | DDC 305.235—dc23/eng/20230517
LC record available at https://lccn.loc.gov/2023021545
LC ebook record available at https://lccn.loc.gov/2023021546

ISBN: 978-1-032-43768-2 (hbk)
ISBN: 978-1-032-43767-5 (pbk)
ISBN: 978-1-003-36877-9 (ebk)

DOI: 10.4324/9781003368779

Typeset in Times New Roman
by codeMantra

We dedicate this book to the hundreds of Lewis & Clark College Graduate students who contributed their stories and experiences to this book, and to the thousands of David Douglas School District students and school professionals we have had the pleasure of working with and learning from for these many years.

Contents

Tables and Figures

Tables

Figures

Introduction & Overview

How can we help adolescents belong (without losing themselves in the herd) and also be themselves (without losing contact with supportive others)? Our effort to provide an answer to this question is the central animating concern of this book. This curriculum is based on our experience running over 300 groups with adolescents over the past ten years as part of a collaborative project between the professors and students of Lewis & Clark College's Graduate School of Education and Counseling (located in Portland, Oregon, USA) and a local, diverse, high-needs, public, middle school (e.g. non-white majority school population, 85% free and reduced lunch, over 50 languages spoken).

What we offer in this curriculum is three-fold, corresponding with the three major sections of the text. In Part One of the text, we provide a conceptual and practical way of understanding two related things: first, the critical leadership challenges faced by group counselors as well as the skills they need to navigate those challenges successfully, and second, the critical developmental challenges faced by adolescents and the skills they need to navigate those challenges successfully. This overall section is grounded in a dialectical framework that we detail at the outset.

In Part Two, we provide a "tried and true" nine-week, social skills curriculum – *Belong and Be You* – that we have designed and modified over the years in our efforts to help adolescents be better socially connected as well as confidently independent. In this section, we provide a full description of each session based on our experience which is meant to be read in advance and provides a richly detailed account and examples of what each session looks and feels like in practice. We also include brief instructions for each session, a summary and outline of the tasks, and materials needed for quick reference on the day each session will be facilitated.

In Part Three of this text, we provide an additional resource which is meant to be used in tandem with the curriculum: We provide a collection of 40 "strategic stories" on four different themes which have been contributed by Lewis & Clark Graduate School faculty and students and have been used as a significant part of the curriculum (described in Part Two). These strategic stories can be used "as is" in any *Belong and Be You* counseling group, but are also provided as inspirational examples of how a group leader can construct their own strategic stories for use in groups.

Overall, our hope is that this text and curriculum provide both a foundation from which to confidently do the work of leading a counseling group for adolescents and a kind of inspiration for how a group leader can adapt and modify the recommendations in this text to particular settings. In the next section, we use the metaphor of running a rapid in a river to describe the dialectical challenges faced by group leaders as they run counseling groups, and adolescents as they navigate their teen years. We want this overall text to be a kind of guidebook, a map of the river, so to speak, which notes both the challenging rapids and the calm moments of reflection and beauty. We hope that group leaders, new and experienced, can use this text to successfully navigate group leadership, and to help adolescents successfully navigate how to both *Belong and Be You.*

Conceptual & Practical Preparation

Navigating Four Important Dialectics in Group Leadership & Navigating Three Important Dialectics in Adolescent Developmental

Overview

In Part One of the text, we provide a conceptual and practical way of understanding two related things: first, the critical leadership challenges faced by group counselors as well as the skills they need to navigate those challenges successfully, and second, the critical developmental challenges faced by adolescents and the skills they need to navigate those challenges successfully. This overall section is grounded in a dialectical framework that we detail at the outset.

DOI: 10.4324/9781003368779-1

Navigating Four Important Dialectics in Group Leadership

Overview

This chapter summarizes the critical leadership challenges faced by group counselors as well as the skills they need to navigate those challenges successfully. An overarching theoretical frame concerning the dialectical view of group leadership is discussed which reflects the ongoing process of self-regulation that a group leader must be able to model. The four major dialectical challenges that a group counselor must navigate in order to lead a group successfully are presented. These dialectical challenges are presented as a kind of map of the river, a kind of description of the rapids that group counselors tend to face in their work, and how we can make our way through these challenges successfully.

As noted in the introduction above, we have supervised our graduate students as they have facilitated over 300 middle school counseling groups over the past ten years. Each year, we have revised the curriculum of these counseling groups based on what we have learned from the last term. This book then represents the culmination of our efforts to not only teach group counseling skills to adults but also help the teens in those counseling groups strengthen their social connections, as well as their individual resilience and identity. Whether we are working with adults in training or adolescents in counseling groups, we hold a common theoretical orientation related to a dialectical approach. In our work with teens, we often begin with a story – a strategic story – that we tell for a reason (more on this later in this section). Here is a story from Peter to introduce the concept of a dialectical approach:

> When I first moved to Oregon, I got excited about learning how to kayak down rivers and through rapids. Early on in my kayaking lessons, some friends took me on a trip to the Deschutes River where I quickly learned that I was in way over my head, literally. I kept trying to paddle through big waves like a grimacing madman and my boat would inevitably flip before I got through the rapid. I would then swim to shore drenched and demoralized.
>
> As we approached one of the biggest rapids named Boxcar, I decided to stick close to an expert named Kelly who was paddling in front of me. We both

DOI: 10.4324/9781003368779-2

sped up as we got to the edge of the big rapid. At that moment, it became clear to me that there was extreme danger on both sides of me: On the left side of the river there was a set of gnarly rocks that clearly needed to be avoided at all costs. On the right side of the river was a huge wave that dropped into a deep and devastating hole of churning white water. I started panicking and paddling too hard in an effort to find a safe line through. I looked up just in time to see Kelly as she calmly took one, smooth, stroke that positioned her boat perfectly to ride right down the ribbon of relatively calm water in the center section of the river. I followed her as best I could. I still swam, but I did get through alive.

The reason why I'm telling you this story is that I think that both the journey of adolescence and the journey of leading groups for adolescents are a lot like the journey down a river that contains rapids. In both cases, adults and teens are faced with challenging choices that must be navigated successfully. Also in both cases, it helps to hold a dialectical view: The successful navigation of rapids is most often found in the clear understanding of the extremes, and in the wisdom to choose the most helpful path through those extremes. Sometimes you need to move over to one side of the river to pick up a little speed, sometimes you need to move toward the calmer side of the river to help things slow down a bit. There is often real danger in going too far to either side in these tumultuous passages, but knowing your full range of options and being able to use all those options is key to finding a safe way through.

The reason a dialectical view is important for group leadership is because it reflects the ongoing process of self-regulation that a group leader should be able to model. If we are too firm and fierce, for example, we risk shutting adolescents down and we lose their liveliness and engagement. If we are too warm and fuzzy and supportive, the teens may consider us "soft" and they will not feel safe or protected by us from the dangers of group participation, such as snarky comments or snide asides within the group. Group leadership is therefore about modeling how to navigate as we lead. In effect, we are modeling what it is like to have a good internal thermostat: we can move between warm and supportive or cool and clear as the temperature in the room and the demands of our role as group leader dictates.

We have found that there are four major dialectical challenges that a group counselor must navigate in order to lead a group successfully. We came to understand these challenges, and the skills inherent in taking on these challenges, through our observations of hundreds of group counselors in training over the past ten years. We share them here as a kind of map of the river, a kind of description of the rapids that group counselors tend to face in their work, and how we can make our way through these challenges successfully. These four dialectical challenges, and the skills that are required for successful navigation of them, are outlined in Table 1. In the sections that follow, we expand on each of the four sets of dialectical skills and provide an example from our curriculum which demonstrates how we use these dialectical skills in practice.

Table 1 The Four Dialectical Skill Sets for Group Leaders

Dialectical Skills	Description	Examples
1 Integration & Differentiation	Counselor helps group members gain both a stronger sense of self and a solid sense of belonging to the group	• facilitates individual voice, participation, identity & • helps group members see, respect, include others
2 Support & Challenge	Counselor provides adequate levels of both warm support as well as appropriate challenge	• empathy, universalizing, active listening, warmth & • fierceness, blocking, questioning, confrontation
3 Direct & Indirect	Counselor demonstrates skills in utilizing both direct and indirect methods of engaging students	• inviting a student to speak, addressing conflict & • creating playful/ imaginative games and activities
4 Personal & Professional	Counselor appropriately negotiates personal & professional boundaries in practice	• use of well-edited "strategic stories" and disclosure & • ability to assume a professional role in context

The Four Dialectical Skill Sets for Group Leaders

Integration & Differentiation: Helping Adolescents Belong and Be Themselves

Belong and Be You is both the title of this curriculum and a description of our two main goals in running these groups: we want the adolescents we work with to both feel more connected to others and strengthen their own identity and re-silience as individuals. Thus, helping teens both integrate with others and dif-ferentiate from others is the main dialectical skill set necessary for group leaders who use this curriculum. This, of course, is no easy task. Group leaders face an inherent challenge in every moment of every session they lead: How much to highlight the individual voices and identities within the group versus how much to work on group cooperation and solidarity as they move through the curriculum? How often does the group leader allow one voice, for example, to be heard above others in the group? Also, how long does the group leader allow a significantly silent member of the group to remain silent before urging or encouraging the individual to join the fray?

As in the metaphor of the river rapids, group counselors need to understand that going too far in one direction with any of these four dialectical challenges is dangerous and limiting. It is equally dangerous, however, to not be able to utilize the full range of skills described in the dialectics. Therefore, truly skilled group leaders find a way to encourage students to both differentiate from each other in small ways early in the group sessions (being able to state, for example, "I like dogs, but not cats.") and in large ways later in the group sessions (being willing to say, for example, "I'm gay and I speak two languages, too."). In this way, the dialectical challenge of integration & differentiation encourages group leaders to work on two goals simultaneously, weaving back and forth like a skillful kayaker on the river, navigating the extremes and finding a way down the river successfully.

An exercise from the first week of the curriculum that we call the "60-Second Autobiography" is an example of how we put into practice the related dialectical skills of both integration and differentiation. As we will detail in the upcoming full description of the first session, we create a game-like atmosphere when facilitating the "60-Second Autobiography" in which students introduce themselves to each other for the first time. We fully understand the challenge of asking an adolescent to introduce themselves in an authentic and unguarded way in front of other adolescents that they may not know. We want these teens to be able to say enough about themselves that they can begin to be known, be integrated, into this newly forming group. But we don't want them to have to stick their necks out too far and make themselves too vulnerable, too differentiated, in a group of strangers.

To accomplish navigation of this challenging dialectic, we create a structure around the "60-Second Autobiography" that makes it less risky. First, we introduce the activity as a game ("We are each going to introduce our whole life story in 60 seconds. Impossible right?"). We also make sure that the structure of the game is clearly defined to limit how much we are asking of them and to make it feel safer for them to engage ("This is a list of all the topics written on this piece of paper that you can try and cover: Pets, People, Places, Play, and Preferences. The timer will beep when your 60 seconds is up and if you have time left over, we will ask you questions to fill the time."). Lastly, we provide clear roles and expectations for group members ("The person to your left will tell you one thing they learned about you and the person on your right will ask you one follow up question."). With this clear structure we are optimizing the extent to which every student gets both integrated into the group (by being heard, acknowledged, and responded to) as well as differentiated from others (by stating some of the facts of their particular lives regarding pets they may have, family configurations they experience, and things they may like to do on a Saturday afternoon.)

As with the "60-Second Autobiography," most of our group activities in this curriculum are used to help accomplish our twin goals in these groups: We want our students to experience both a sense of real connection to others as well as to experience a strongly independent and resourceful sense of self, and we want these two related experiences to deepen over the nine sessions of the group. The following sets of dialectical skills all support this primary goal set.

Support & Challenge: Creating Safety & Protecting the Group with Fierceness

The image of navigating through a river rapid has many parallels with group leadership. As with all metaphors, however, the parallels are not complete: The map does not completely fit the actual terrain. For example, when navigating the rapid called "Boxcar" that was described above, both the big rocks and the big river hole were clearly to be avoided. In our way of thinking about dialectical group leadership skills, the tension we are trying to navigate is between two important and necessary skills that are tied to a common outcome. Any one of these skills used to the extreme is not helpful, but understanding and being able to use them both demonstrates a full "range of motion" that group leaders need to effective. In this way, another dialectically-related metaphor can be borrowed from the discipline of physical therapy where the goal is to have a complete and unrestricted "range of motion" in our muscle groups and joints: We want our arms to be able to open wide to welcome someone in for a hug, but also want to be able to cross our arms tightly across our chests when we are cold or threatened.

The dialectical skills of being able to offer warm support to our students while at the same time being firm about behavioral expectations and fierce in our defense of group safety is a great example of the importance of this "range of motion." We have found unfortunately, that group leadership skills are most often described inaccurately as a discrete set of single skills that lean heavily toward what we would call the "warm and supportive" end of this continuum (e.g. reflecting, summarizing, linking, unconditional regard, etc.) and hardly recognizing the need for those on the other end of the dialectical continuum related to "challenge and fierceness" (e.g. directing, blocking, energizing, confronting, etc.).

We have come to see the dialectical skills of "Support & Challenge" as necessarily related in a very important way: They are both necessary to create a safe group that is able to develop in complexity over time. Here is a specific example of what we mean: It is understandable that the teens come into a new group experience wary and self-protective. Their school hallways are often filled with eye rolls, verbal taunts, and bullying behaviors. We can't expect these students to suddenly feel safe in our small group settings just because we say it will be in a warm and inviting way. Too often, we have seen group leaders use their biggest smiles, their nicest words, and their warmest gestures to communicate to the students that "this group will be a safe space," only to be met by snarky comments and impatient sighs of disbelief. We think we know why: The students know that all the leader's kind words and intentions are not going to protect them from the humiliation of potentially being laughed at if they let down their guard. To counter this understandable resistance to engaging authentically in the group counseling experience, we encourage our leaders to draw from the "challenge" end of the dialectic and to let the students know through word and action that they will be fiercely protecting the individuals in the group from any subtle slights or overt slams.

In the first session of one of our groups, for example, group leader Rachel faced a particularly challenging, yet very subtle moment but was able to address it with a helpful assertiveness. Rachel was gently checking in with the students about how their transition to middle school was going. Not far into the session, one boy named Charles shyly admitted to forgetting his locker combination multiple times during the first week of school. Another boy, Cayman, rolled his eyes and scoffed under his breath in a clear critique of what he perceived as Charles's ineptitude.

Without a clear intention to use "fierceness" as a group leader, Rachel may have let this moment pass with a small and reassuring gesture of support to Charles (e.g. "Wow, Charles, that must have been a challenging moment!"). For his part, Charles would have been left with a clear message of support from his group leader, but also with a clear message of scorn and dismissal from his classmate. With this kind of glossy response, Rachel would have been only leaning on the set of "cooperative" or "supportive" skills that all group leaders learn in their training. Instead, because of her explicit training that such challenging moments may require an equally challenging response from her to restore safety in the group, Rachel was able to respond with a helpfully "fierce" statement that sent a clear message to her young charges. Just after she noticed Cayman roll his eyes and scoff at Charles's admission of personal shame, Rachel leaned into the group physically, making no direct eye contact with either Cayman or Charles, and stated the following:

> As leader of this group, just to let everyone know up front, I want to make it clear that this is going to be a safe group. We will not be allowing put downs of any kind as we work together. You know what put downs are? Put downs can include anything like making fun of another person with words, or even just rolling your eyes after they say something. Although I know these things go on all the time outside of here, in the halls, the playground, on the bus, I want to make it clear that in here, in this group, it's not going to happen. In support of what Charles said, how many of you forgot your locker combination or even just felt awkward during your first week of school?

In our view, Rachel's response accomplished something very important, and somewhat paradoxical, in the first session of her group: Although she did not (importantly, more on this later) confront Cayman specifically, everyone in that group got the message that there was someone in charge of that group who would be actively working to keep it a safe place. If Rachel has not assertively and, we would argue, fiercely addressed Cayman's seemingly small, bullying-type behavior, Charles, and everyone else in the group, would have quickly learned that the group was not in fact a safe place to be. With Rachel's fierce moment, the group did, however learn they could relax a bit: Someone who was both nice, and fierce, was in charge. Navigating the dialectical skill set of support and challenge is closely related, in our view, to what research has found to be the most effective parenting style. That is, we encourage our group leaders to be neither too permissive in their leadership style, nor too authoritarian. Instead, we encourage them to demonstrate both support and challenge as they develop an authoritative "both/and" style of leadership.

Direct & Indirect: Addressing Conflict & Making Animal Cards

In the example above, we stressed the importance of how Rachel did not look directly at Cayman when she made her "fierce" move to protect the group. This is an example of a leader using an "indirect" style of confrontation that we have found effective with adolescents: Challenging an adolescent directly in a group often leads to an escalating power struggle within that group. Instead, we encourage our group leaders to take on challenging behaviors and difficult issues with a combination of both direct and indirect approaches. If a student has been acting up in group, for example, we encourage the leader to walk next to that student as they make their way to group or back to class and take that opportunity to have a "side-by-side" conversation (i.e. indirectly) in which they check in with the student to see how things are going from their perspective, but also to reinforce expectations and consequences for behavior in the group (i.e. directly). Similarly, if a student is consistently taking up a lot of verbal space in the group, we may use that "side by side" conversation to remind them that there are low talkers in the group who need practice speaking up and high talkers in the group that might need practice letting others contribute (a dialectical way of looking at high and low talkers…).

There is another important dimension to using both direct and indirect approaches in groups with adolescents. In the section above, we described the paradoxical effect of creating group safety by being willing as a leader to demonstrate fierceness as well as warmth and support. We have also found a paradoxical effect related to the dialectical skill set of direct and indirect work: Many times, the students in our groups will say the most direct things about themselves when they are not talking directly about themselves. Here are some examples: We might ask them to use the metaphor of a weather report (in Session 3) to check in on how they have been doing that week. We might also ask them to respond to the metaphor of the bear (in Session 4) as a way of talking about strong emotions that all of us experience. After hearing a strategic story about bullying from their group leader's own experience (in Session 5) we might also ask the students what they noticed in that story, which often leads directly back to the students' own experiences. These examples of how indirect approaches allow a paradoxically more direct response from the students seem to be related to the "support/challenge" dialectic described above: Indirect approaches seem to offer support for the students to take on the challenge of addressing real issues in their own lives.

One particular application of this "indirect-to-direct" approach is reflected in our use of *Animal Cards* (in Sessions 3 and 9). These are a stack of over 100, laminated images of animals that we cut out and laminate for use in multiple sessions of *Belong and Be You*. Although the ways we use these cards will be described in more detail in the weekly session outlined below, we suggest you create a stack of these cards yourself before the group begins. In the paragraphs below, we describe how.

Inspired by the Gestalt Play Therapy approach pioneered by Violet Oaklander (Oaklander, 1978, Mortola, 2003, 2006), we collect images of animals from all sorts of sources, including magazines, calendars, and old books (There are also handy photo essay book full of high quality and consistently-sized images on various themes). In choosing the images of animals, we look for some that carry some obvious emotional weight (e.g. a lion with teeth bared, a colorful butterfly in a peaceful meadow, a bear hugging a cub, etc.). We also choose some which are ambiguous and open to interpretation (e.g. beads of dew on a spider's web, a hyena laughing, two wolves circling each other, etc.). Our goal is to collect a wide range of images that captures many aspects of animal life including being solo, being in a group, defending territory, relaxing, playing, hiding, doing something challenging, etc. These images have an easily recognized parallel with human experience, but mediated "indirectly" through the life and worlds of animals. In our work, we find that many children find these images of animals easy to relate to as they work to express their own life experiences.

Once we have a broad collection of these images (we suggest at least 100), we either cut them to a consistent size (approximately 4 × 6 inches or larger) and paste or tape them back-to-back. Alternatively, we create a set of colorful construction paper cards (also approximately 4 × 6 inches or larger) and paste the images of animals onto these cards, both front and back (this use of construction paper allows more flexibility in the size of the animal images you can use). We then laminate these cards, which we have found to be a key step for both longevity and also "shiny" attractiveness. In recent years, fairly inexpensive home laminators have become available which we have purchased and use often in creating sets of lovely, laminated, image cards. We have used these laminators to also create many other themed sets of images: We have sets of "people cards" with diverse images from cultures around the world, "nature cards" with many evocative scenes from landscapes in nature, and specific sets of "cat" and "dog" cards, all of which we have used in our work with children and adolescents. For simplicity purposes regarding the *Belong and Be You* curriculum, we have limited our use of these creative sets to just the *Animal Cards*, to great effect.

Sometimes, we keep these finished *Animal Cards* in an old metal box that looks like it could be holding treasure. We have found that this heightens the child's or adolescent's interest and engagement with them. Because of the lovely slick surface of the cards created by the lamination, we can toss a stack of them across the floor and they will spread out like a deck of playing cards. This dramatic touch also seems to enhance their appeal. When the cards are all spread out across the floor in a colorful and chaotic collage, it's difficult for teens to resist rooting through them. Once they start the search for the cards that best fit them at that moment, they become deeply involved in the process of projecting their own experience onto the cards. Paradoxically, this "indirect" process therefore helps them to be aware of and in touch with their own emotions, thoughts, and experiences as they shuffle through a random pile of images of animals.

We have used our *Animal Cards* with both individuals and groups. As a kind of "check in" at the beginning of a session we might say, "Pick a card or two to represent how you are feeling today." They can also be used in other helpful ways (e.g. "pick a card to represent everyone in your family/friend group."), as well as a way to help close the group altogether in the last session. In the descriptions of the weekly sessions below, we provide more specific details of how we use this effective "indirect" method to help the individuals in our groups both speak about their own experiences, as well as finding ways they connect with others.

Personal & Professional: Making Strategic Stories & Collecting Group Data

When running groups with adolescents, there are obvious personal boundaries that must be respected between the group leaders and the students (including physical, emotional, and social boundaries). There are also important professional boundaries that we need to respect given the context of our groups in schools (including the bell schedule, norms and rules for student behavior, and fingerprinting and background checks for our group leaders). As we have stated, we recognize the danger of going "too far" in either direction regarding these dialectical skill sets. In the case of negotiating the dialectical skill set of personal & professional, we recognize the danger of a group leader bringing too much personal material into the counseling context with adolescents, which would breach important boundaries. We also recognize that if a leader only presents themselves as a rigid, professional authority, then much of the authentic life of a group can be squeezed out.

We think it is important to recognize the group leader's role as a model of the kind of behavior we expect in these groups. Just as a teacher in a classroom needs to model what it is like to be a good learner, it is important that a group counselor is able to model key aspects of what we want our students to gain in the group counseling experience, such as appropriate personal disclosure, the ability to demonstrate emotional regulation, and the willingness to work through difficult interpersonal experiences. In this section, we will describe key examples of both the personal end of the dialectic as well as the professional end. As an example of how to bring the self of the counselor appropriately into the process and curriculum of group counseling, we will describe how we use strategic storytelling in four out of nine of the *Belong and Be You* sessions that follow. We will also describe the important process of data collection within the group as a way to address professional accountability as a group leader.

Using Strategic Storytelling

Strategic storytelling was first described in *BAM! Boys Advocacy and Mentoring* (Mortola et al., 2008), a curriculum specifically designed for running boys' groups. This present curriculum focuses on groups that include all genders but we find strategic storytelling to be just as helpful. Each year, when we lead these groups in schools, the moment that most often heralds the groups' movement into the "working stage" is when one of the group leaders shares their first strategic story. We generally don't share a strategic story with the students until Session 4, when the appropriate groundwork has been laid and the group cohesion is strong enough to start addressing some challenging content.

In brief, a strategic story is a story gleaned from the counselor's own lived experience that directly addresses the content of the curriculum for that week. As will be detailed in the session descriptions, in Session 4 we use a strategic story to address emotional regulation. In Session 5, we use a story to address some aspects of bullying. In Session 6, we use a story to address the costs and benefits of belonging, and in Session 7 we use a strategic story to explore issues of "being you," identity, and being unique.

The function of these stories is multi-layered: At the most basic layer, the stories help us introduce the content of the week in a compelling and "complexifying" way. We know the students have repeatedly heard about how to control one's emotions or address bullying, for example. We want, therefore, to use a story to "indirectly" engage their interest and also to allow them to think and feel in new and appropriately complex ways regarding the content. Emotions, bullying, belonging, and being unique are not easy or simple issues and, in fact, are often addressed in our relationships throughout the life-span. We want to address these issues through strategic stories, therefore, that allow us to highlight the many facets of the issue. We have seen these strategic stories be very effective in getting the students to "lean into" the experience of openly listening while the leader is sharing, becoming quietly attentive and thoughtfully engaged, sometimes with their mouths agape, just like they were little ones at story time.

Another important layer regarding the use of strategic storytelling has to do with what we model in the telling of these stories. While the students are watching the group leader tell this story, they are witnessing someone get in touch with a challenging incident with all kinds of emotions involved. The students are also witnessing someone be able to put this challenging incident into words, and, additionally, to work through the emotions involved and reflect on that experience. These are the very skills that want the students to be able to demonstrate themselves. What we tend to see happen after a leader shares a strategic story is that, soon after, the students themselves are more willing to jump into the challenging subject matter with ideas and incidents from their own experience. These stories also provide grounded examples and language to describe abstract concepts we want the students to understand and grapple with, such as "mindfulness," "relational aggression," "microaggressions," or "identity development."

As we highlighted in the section above, strategic stories also allow us to address these difficult subjects with an indirect approach: We start with an example from the leader's own life, and more often than not, we end up hearing of multiple examples from the student's own lives, even those who have been reluctant to share in past weeks. We do need to be careful in sharing these stories to not step over inappropriate boundaries, but we have seen them be very effective in engaging our students in addressing challenging topics.

The guidelines for making a good strategic story are as follows: The content should be real enough that it rings true for the students who listen, but it should also be content that has been "worked through" in the leader's own life to a great extent. It is okay to tell a story, for example, of losing a group of friends, and even to feel emotions related to that loss, but the leader should not be overwhelmed by emotion in the telling, and the students should not be pulled into a caretaking role as listeners. We recommend that leaders tell potential stories repeatedly to other trusted adults, working through the details and telling so it is clear why they are telling it and how to tell it most effectively.

We have found that it is most helpful if the strategic stories contain a common structure: They start out with a set of interesting details about a specific time and place and a bit about who the leader was at the time ("I was raised in a large family with 8 siblings and I was always wearing hand-me-downs because we didn't have much money…"). The story then moves toward a particular incident that embodies the content at the heart of the week's curriculum ("One day, after I went shopping with my own money that I had earned and bought 3 pairs of new jeans, my dad made me return them all…"). Ultimately, we suggest that the leader adds a third part to the story which begins with the phrase, "The reason I am telling you this story is because…" ("I'm telling you this story because I know how hard it can be to try and develop your own individuality in some families and that is something I still work on in my own life.")

Importantly, after the story is told to the students, the first question we ask is, "I'm curious, what stood out to you from the story?" The reason we ask this question is linked to the section on direct/indirect approaches above. We have found that very direct prompts such as, "Has anything like this ever happened to you?" are not helpful. More often than not, such a direct prompt shuts the students down. By allowing them to answer the more indirect question of what stood out, more often than not, we hear very direct statements of how the content of the story links to their own experience (e.g. "When you talked about the jeans, I was thinking of how everyone at this school has to have fancy shoes, but my family can't afford them.") We quote from the *BAM!* Curriculum (2008) below for more on what makes a good strategic story:

> Story telling is more effective when the stories are rich in detail. Before telling a story, picture the scene in your mind. What were the sights, sounds, and smells of the time? When you tell a story from your own experience, we recommend you use names for the characters in the story, describe the settings, recall the street names. Tell it as if it were happening now. The more you can be present in the telling, the more the children will be present in their listening. Lean in toward them, use hand gestures, change the pace, the pitch, and the rhythm of your voice. Practice your story ahead of time to hear the parts of the story that are most powerful at creating contact. Notice when your listeners are giving you their best attention. Use humor and have fun!
>
> (p. 24)

We consider strategic stories to be important enough in this work that we have collected 40 sample strategic stories from our group leaders over the years (receiving their permission to share them anonymously) and have included them in four sections (managing emotions, addressing bullying, finding belonging, and being unique) in Part Three of this book. These example stories could be of use in your own groups as they are, or they can serve as a springboard for you to come up with ideas for your own stories. Additionally, in order to begin to mine your own experience for incidents that could be turned into strategic stories of your own, we suggest you read through the following exercise, take notes, make drawings of your own schoolyard, and see what comes up. Ultimately, these strategic stories, though tough to remember and perhaps relive, are an opportunity for us to turn the difficult lemons of our own experience into lemonade that will nourish and help the young lives of the students in our groups.

> In your mind's eye, imagine where you used to eat lunch when you were in a grade somewhere between fifth grade and high school. Where do you sit for lunch? What did you tend to have to eat? Can you remember the kinds of foods other kids used to eat? Who did you sit with? Can you remember different groups of kids who sat together during lunch? Where did you fit in with those groups? Were you the kind of kid that had one or two good friends, or did you tend to hang out with a larger group of friends? Can you remember anything about the "pecking order" that might have existed at your school? If so, who were the popular kids and who might be the less popular kids? Which particular kids were very much on the margins socially? Who were those kids? What did they tend to get teased, bullied or ostracized for? Did any of them have allies who supported them?
>
> More generally at that age, were there particular kids that were very much "on the top of the heap" socially speaking? How did they use their power to

include or exclude? What made them popular and what kinds of things were very much socially valued at your school? (e.g. shoes, clothing, looks, money, race, language, etc.) Can you remember any particular incidents where a child was bullied by another child or by a group? If so, what was the bullying about and what, if any, was your own role in that incident? (e.g. were you the aggressor, the aggressed upon, or a kind of bystander?) Can you also remember any particular incidents where you or other kids got really angry, had a fight, cried or got really embarrassed at school? Which emotions were part of that incident and how were those feelings expressed, denied, and/or managed? How did other kids or adults react to that emotion being expressed? How were you taught to address your emotions? What might have been more helpful?

When you were at recess or after school, what kinds of activities did you participate in? What were you good at and what were not so good at? Did you find it easy or more difficult to join in the kinds of activities that were popular back then? More broadly, what kinds of activities were you drawn to after school, on weekends, or during summer? Did you tend toward more active things (like sports or games) or were you on the quieter, more introspective end of the spectrum (reading, video games, etc.)? During school, in which subjects were you good and in which ones did you struggle? How did those strengths/challenges influence who you became later in life?

What were some ways in which you felt a sense of both belonging (e.g. family, church, clubs, sports, nature, etc.) and uniqueness (e.g. culture, identity, race, difference, language, hobbies, learning styles, etc.) during those years? How did you find out about the ways you were different or unique and how easy was it to embrace that difference? What are the ways you felt a strong sense of kinship with others (or with pets, animals or nature) and how helpful was that to you growing up? Did you ever struggle with holding the balance between "being your own person" and "being part of the group"? How did you resolve those issues over time?

Collecting Group Data Regarding Group Goals

In the previous section, we used strategic storytelling as an example of how we can dive, thoughtfully, into our personal experience to benefit the lives of the students in our groups. In this section on data collection, we provide an example of the ways we can use our professional role as conscientious and thoughtful group counselors to learn from data about what works best for our students in our work with them.

As professionals in this area of mental health with adolescents, we are often asked to be clear on the goals we set for the individuals and groups with whom we work. Additionally, we are asked to be able to demonstrate how effective our work is in reaching those stated goals. We have honed our goals for this curriculum and these groups over the years we have been using it, learning more about what our true focus and intention is with these groups. As a result, we have come up with three primary outcomes we work toward with the students in their school environment:

1 to increase social connections and supportive relationships in and outside the group
2 to increase acceptance and respect of individual differences and identities in and outside the group
3 to increase skills and options to address various forms of bullying in and outside the group

Over the nine weeks while our groups are running, we collect three kinds of data in order to understand how successful we are meeting these goals and also to better understand our participant's experience in the groups: *pre- and post-assessments*, *weekly surveys*, and various *qualitative data.*

Pre- and Post-Assessment

The first kind of data we collect is a *pre- and post-assessment* which we ask the participants to fill out at the end of the first and last sessions of the group. The *pre- and post-assessment*, a version of which is included in Table 2, gives us a sense of the overall movement of our participants in relation to the goals we have set for the group. As you can see, the questions on the *pre- and post-assessment* are aligned with the goals of the group described above.

We have found over time that the data results from the pre- and post-assessment generally indicate that the student responses to the questions change positively from the pre-test to the post-test. That is, our groups help the students move positively toward the goals we have set for the groups in that they generally feel better connected to others, stronger in their own sense of self, and better equipped to address bullying in their lives.

Weekly Surveys

The second kind of data we collect is a *weekly survey*, a version of which is included in Table 3. We ask the participants to fill out the *weekly survey* at the end of each session, including the first and last sessions when they are also filling out the *pre- and post-assessments*. The *weekly survey* allows us to see, over time, and week-to-week, how they respond, as individuals and as a group, to the different aspects of this curriculum.

We have used the data from these *weekly surveys* to modify, tweak, and adapt this curriculum over the years. In this way, the *weekly surveys* have provided us a rich source of feedback. The data from the *weekly survey* taught us, for example, that we needed to more slowly introduce the more serious content of the curriculum and allow for more support in the group to be established in the early weeks. The *weekly survey* also allows us to understand how each member

Table 2 Pre- and Post-Assessment Example

Pre- & Post-Test Name: Age: Gender: Ethnicity: Leaders:	*1.* *Strongly* *Disagree*	*2.* *Disagree*	*3.* *Not* *Sure*	*4.* *Agree*	*5.* *Strongly* *Agree*
1 I am able to empathize & appreciate others' perspectives or point of views					
2 I feel connected to my classmates when I come to school					
3 I feel like I can be myself around my classmates					
4 I respect and accept others who are different from me					
5 I can identify strategies and steps to handle a bullying situation					
6 I only hang out with people who are similar to me					
7 I feel like bullying is taken seriously in my school					
8 I have the skills to stand up for myself when I am being bullied					

Comments:

Table 3 Weekly Survey Example

Week Name:	*1.* *Not at all* ☹	*2.* *Not* *much*	*3.* *Some what* 🙂	*4.* *Yes I* *did*	*5.* *Very much* 😄
1 I liked being in group today					
2 I felt connected and respected in my group today					
3 I accepted and respected my group members today					

Today I liked/did not like:

of our group is responding to each weekly session, especially in relation to the responses of the other members of the group, allowing us to tailor specific approaches to specific participants as we go along.

We are also able to use the data we collect from the *pre- and post-assessment* as well as the *weekly survey* to present to stakeholders at the school in which we work (e.g. administrators, teachers, parents, and the participants themselves) to show the overall positive experience the participants are having in the groups and therefore the positive effect we are having by offering these groups. For example, in the graph for Table 4, we are able to very simply show the data which summarizes the responses of 60 participants in 15 groups that we ran one term for nine weeks at the middle school. The solid lower line in the graph represents the mean average responses of all participants to the four questions we ask in the *weekly survey* after Week 1 of the curriculum. The dashed, upper line shows these same averages of the four questions in the *weekly survey* collected after Week 9 of the curriculum. We are able to show, in this way, that all 15 of the groups we ran were collectively able to demonstrate more positive responses on the *weekly surveys* after Week 9 than they did after Week 1. Because the questions on the *weekly surveys* are based on our group goals, we can therefore use this kind of data to show some success in moving toward our group goals over the nine weeks of the curriculum.

Another example of how the *weekly survey* data can be useful is reflected in the graph in Table 5. This graph shows the average responses of one group's participants for each of the nine weeks regarding the statement: "I felt connected and respected in group today." Two important aspects of the group participants' personal and collective experience are represented in this data: One, the overall averages for this group regarding this important question show a general rise over time, reflecting how participants generally felt more "connected and respected" as the group progressed. Two, there was a distinct "dip" in Week 5,

Table 4 Overall Comparison of Weeks 1 & 9 – Weekly Surveys

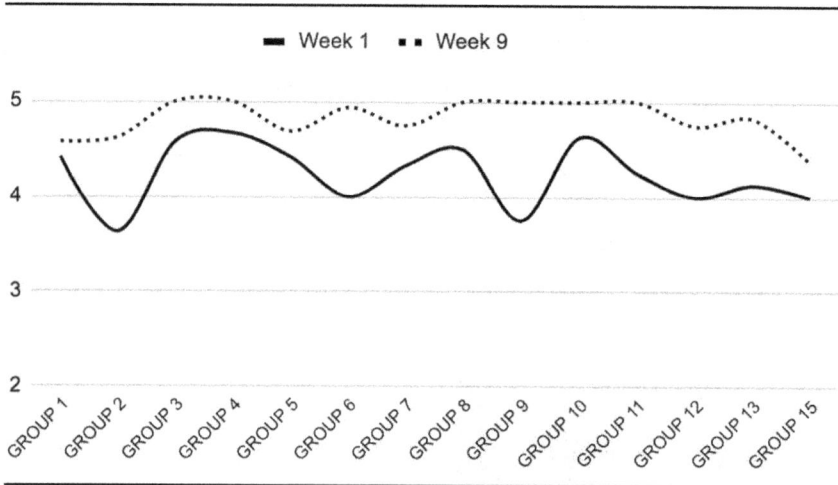

Table 5 Responses to One Question Over Time – Weekly Surveys

"I Felt Connected and Respected in Group Today"

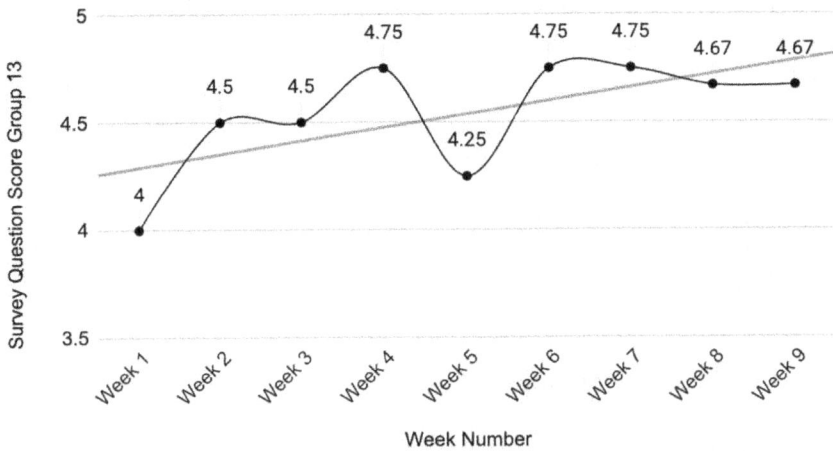

which is the week we begin to address issues of bullying in the school. Because of this challenging and sometimes triggering content, many students understandably find Session 5 challenging. Digging a bit deeper, we can also make sense of this dip for Session 5 by noting how one student in the group that week very much wanted to draw out his feelings (as he had been able to do so the prior week using the "Personal Weather Report"). The student was disappointed that the leaders had a different set of activities on the agenda that day. This one student was honest in his assessment of his experience in the group that day and gave a lower-than-average score, which he thoughtfully explained to the leaders later.

Qualitative Data

We also collect various kinds of qualitative data throughout the nine sessions. These types of data are generally a combination of images and statements shared by the participants as part of their engagement in tasks outlined in the curriculum. For example, as we described in the "Direct & Indirect" dialectic section above, we often use *Animal Cards* as a way to have participants talk about their personal experience in an indirect way. One example of how we use *Animal Cards* as a kind of qualitative data that we collect is the *Closing Card* activity in the ninth and last session of the group. On this same day when they are giving us pieces of quantitative data in the form of the last weekly survey as well as the post-assessment, we also ask them to engage in an activity that provides us with rich qualitative data that in some ways more powerfully describes their experience in the group than the numbers represented on the assessments and surveys.

In the *Closing Card* activity, we ask the students to pick three images from a large stack of the *Animal Cards*. The first image we ask them to pick is to

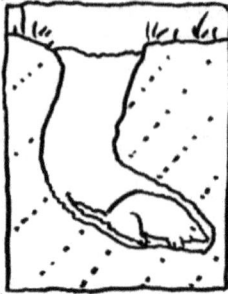

"Before group, I didn't even know any of you. I was like, who are these people? I do not know them – They are not my kind. I felt like I was hiding."

"Now, I'm starting to ease up. When I really got into group, I was laughing and having fun."

"This card is a bad thing because I don't want group to end. I have my reasons. I look like an anime character contemplating life."

Figure 1 Closing Card Activity Example

represent something about their experience *before the group* started, nine weeks ago. The second image is to represent something about their experience *in the group* over the past nine weeks. Lastly, the third image is to represent something they are *taking from the group* now that it is ending. The images and words shared by one participant and which we show in modified sketches in Figure 1 are an example of the kinds of qualitative data the participants will share when prompted in this activity. Perhaps not surprisingly, the theme of moving from "lonely/isolated" to "connected/together" tends to be the unprompted reply of many participants.

We will outline in the week-by-week descriptions of the curriculum ahead how we use drawings and other "indirect" activities that result in various types of qualitative data from our groups. In tandem with the quantitative data from the pre-post surveys as well as the weekly surveys that we have described above, these qualitative data help us better assess and understand the participants in our groups as we work with them during our sessions together.

References

Mortola, P. (2003). *Talking cards.* In H.G. Kaduson, & C.E. Schaefer (Eds.), *101 favorite play therapy techniques.* Vol. 3, 286–289. Jason Aronson, Inc., Northvale, NJ.

Mortola, P. (2006). *Windowframes: Learning the art of Gestalt play therapy the Oaklander way.* Gestalt Press/Routledge Press, Highland, NY.

Mortola, P., Hiton, H., & Grant, S. (2008). *BAM! Boys advocacy and mentoring: A leader's guide to facilitating strength based groups for boys: Guidebook for leading preventative boys groups.* The Routledge Series on Counseling and Psychotherapy with Men and Boys. Routledge Press, New York.

Oaklander, V. (1978). *Windows to our children: A gestalt therapy approach to children and adolescents.* The Gestalt Journal Press, Highland, NY.

Navigating Three Important Dialectics in Adolescent Developmental

Overview

The last chapter summarized the dialectical challenges of group leadership and identified four sets of related skills that group leaders needed to navigate group leadership successfully. This chapter summarizes the three major developmental challenges or passages of adolescence, the "rapids in the river," the dialectical tensions, that teens must successfully navigate in order to gain a safe passage through this crucially important period of their lives. It also addresses both the possibilities and the potential pitfalls of these developmental passages as well as showing how this understanding of the crucial dialectical tensions of adolescence informed the authors work with them, the curriculum they developed, and the goals they have for this curriculum.

A wealth of recent research and writing about adolescence (please see the reference section for specific authors) has informed how we think about adolescents, how we go about working with them, and what our goals are in the groups that we run with teens. We think it is important to have our work grounded in a clear understanding of adolescence, in a theoretical and research-based framework that can guide our approach to engaging teens and helping them grow. Throughout this section, we refer to "adolescents" and "teenagers" even though we are well aware that the sixth graders we tend to work with are about 12 years old on average. It is important to understand that children this age are in most cases already engaged in the journey of adolescence, as we will describe below. In these sections, we summarize the research we have found most helpful and provide a metaphorical framework to think about the developmental process of adolescence overall.

When framing the dialectical challenges of group leadership above, we identified four sets of related skills that group leaders needed to navigate. In the sections that follow, we will summarize what we see as the three major developmental challenges or passages of adolescence, the "rapids in the river," the dialectical tensions, that teens must successfully navigate in order to gain a safe passage through this crucially important period of their lives. In doing so, we

DOI: 10.4324/9781003368779-3

Table 6 The Three Dialectics of Adolescent Development

Dialectics	Description	Examples
1 Childhood & Adulthood	Adolescent is able to both use the support of "the nest" and begin making moves to "leave the nest."	• asks for help and support when needed & initiates moves toward independence and autonomy
2 Gas pedal & Brakes	Adolescent is able to both assertively use the "gas pedal" and appropriately apply "the brakes."	• demonstrates assertiveness and motivation & • uses discernment in decision-making
3 Affiliation & Status	Adolescent is able to both connect and cooperate with others and develop a strong and resilient "sense of self."	• joins and engages with others in mutual support & • demonstrates unique attributes and identity

address both the possibilities and the potential pitfalls of these developmental passages. We will also show how this understanding of the crucial dialectical tensions of adolescence informs our work with them, the curriculum we have developed, and the goals we have for this curriculum. The three dialectical challenges of adolescence as we see them are detailed in Table 6.

Childhood & Adulthood

The most obvious change in adolescence is the metamorphosis from being a child to becoming an adult. What is not so obvious is how that basic process has changed and shifted in the past few decades. Adolescence is traditionally thought of as beginning in biology and ending in society. That is, puberty is kicked off by biological changes that propel physical, emotional, and intellectual changes in the individual. The point at which adolescence ends has traditionally been decided by society: An individual has been considered an "adult" when they have left the nest, struck out on their own, secured a livelihood, and possibly partnered and parented with another. Important changes at both the beginning and the end of adolescence have emerged over time, however, as described by Goldstein (2011):

> The biological and social phases in the lives of young people are drifting apart ever stronger. While adolescents become adults earlier in a biological sense, they reach adulthood later regarding their social and economic roles.

Over time, the biological influences of adolescence have started earlier. Females in the United States are commencing with menses years earlier than they did a century ago. In his book, the *Age of Opportunity*, Steinberg (2014) describes that "girls today on average are menstruating for the first time around their twelfth birthday, this means that the average American girl is beginning puberty at around age nine..." (p. 50). One effect of this change has been the lengthening of adolescence. On average, females used to begin menses at closer to 15 years of age and leave adolescence by partnering around the age of 20. Now they are biologically starting puberty earlier and taking longer to reach adulthood by partnering later, taking more time to complete schooling, and staying financially dependent on their families, in many cases until they are well into their twenties. Experts now describe adolescence, for both males and females, as lasting more than a decade, from about 12 years old to about 24 years old. This is an important change for both those going into adolescence to know, as well as those who are caretaking them through this passage.

While biological changes in females have a clearer marker to measure the change in the onset of adolescence, there is also evidence that males are beginning puberty earlier as well, though less directly measurable. This change toward an earlier onset of puberty in males can be seen in the fact that the "accident hump" has shifted earlier on average. The accident hump refers to the fact that more males than females tend to have life-threatening accidents occur in the younger phase of their lives, often through risk-taking activities that put them in danger (think about concrete skate parks, fast cars, and tackle football). Over time the accident hump has shifted earlier in adolescence, as described by Goldstein (2011):

> This accident hump coincides with the peak of testosterone over the life cycle and is presumably driven at least part by the male biological life cycle. A shift of the curve to younger ages seems to have occurred over time, either as a result of changing risk conditions...or changing risk-taking behavior.

There are indeed dangers as adolescents attempt to navigate this passage from childhood to adulthood. For one thing, they find themselves in this particular passage for a longer period of time, years longer than those of many of the adults who are now caretakers in their lives. In this way, they have a longer set of rapids to run, so to speak. They have a longer exposure to the perils of early and unwanted pregnancy, for example, or the dangers of head injury as they attempt more and more difficult tricks in the skate park.

In addition to these physical perils, there are also psychological challenges that children face as they make their way through their passage from childhood to adulthood. Steinberg (2014) has detailed how our brains reach their full adult size at about age ten and how very few serious psychological problems occur before that age (exceptions to this rule include ADHD, Separation anxiety disorder, learning disorders, and autism spectrum disorders). When an individual reaches 25 years of age, having successfully completed the passage from childhood to adulthood, the chances they will develop a serious psychological problem later in life are small. It is right in the middle of adolescence, however, in the middle of this first challenging passage from childhood to adulthood, that the risks are highest. Steinberg (2014) states:

> The average age of onset for serious mental health problems is fourteen: Mood disorders, substance abuse disorders, most anxiety disorders, most impulse control disorders, eating disorders, schizophrenia.

This teenage vulnerability for serious psychological disorders is related to the fact that the brain is undergoing substantial changes in organization during this age: As children, our brains are designed to soak up as much new and varied information as possible. In adolescence, our brains begin a necessary "pruning" process to allow us to become focused on and expert in a smaller set of things. This pruning process, however, can "unmask potential problems," states Daniel Siegel (2013) in his book *Brainstorm: The Power and Purpose of the Teenage Brain*, "This is why a number of mental health challenges, like mood difficulties such as depression and bipolar disorder, or thinking difficulties such as schizophrenia, may emerge more in adolescence than in childhood" (p. 98).

Given these physical and psychological vulnerabilities, the passage from childhood to adulthood is clearly fraught with challenges. There does, however, seem to be a "method to the madness" of why teens go through such a period of potential turmoil. Teenagers are not just simply being overly-dramatic and hormonally-challenged, they are helping us evolve as a species. The latest thinking about the function of adolescence is that it provides an extended window of time where new possibilities can be considered, new ways of living can be experimented with, and reality itself can be seen differently. As Siegel (2013) states:

> This period of the teenage years and early twenties is a time of great potential and of great constructive power. The push against traditional ways of doing things and of thinking about reality can yield ways of thinking outside the box that enable new and creative ways of doing things to emerge.

To summarize this section: The first major passage of adolescence is the dramatic move from childhood to adulthood and involves a careful navigation between two extremes. On the one hand, the teen can't simply be untethered from the care and support that should surround them in childhood, nor can they ignore the necessary challenge of leaving some aspects of childhood dependence and security behind. We as adults can help teens through this passage by taking a wise and compassionate view of the challenges of this period, and helping teens themselves view their own situation compassionately and clearly. We can help provide adolescents with a kind of map, a story-line, of the expected terrain their teens will pass through by being informed of the latest research on adolescence and by being able to share this information in helpful ways. Using our own experience detailed in our strategic stories about the bumps we passed through during adolescents are a helpful way to help them see their own experience better. Such stories help contextualize big concepts such as we have attempted to do with our metaphor of river rapids being akin to adolescent passages.

Identifying and describing this first big passage of the teen years – between childhood and adulthood – helps us to answer the question, *"what* is happening in adolescence?" The answer to that, of course, is that the child is becoming an adult. The next big passage of adolescence we describe will help to answer the question *"how* does this change happen?" while the third and last passage we describe will help to answer the question, *"why* does this change happen?"

Gas Pedal & Brakes

As we have written, *what* is happening in adolescence is the movement, the passage, from childhood to adulthood. *How* that passage, this movement, happens is that both biology and society conspire to provide adolescents with a kind of a gas pedal and an engine, metaphorically speaking, to aide them on their journey. This "gas pedal" motivates teenagers from many species, in fact, to take risks, as described by Barbara Natterson-Horowitz and Kathryn Bowers (2013), in their text *Zoobiquity*:

> ...a new pleasure in risk-taking likely propels nearly grown birds out of nests...and human teens into malls and college dorms...the biology of decreased fear, greater interest in novelty, and impulsivity serve a purpose across species...it could be that the only thing more dangerous than risk-taking in adolescence is not taking them.

Teens are therefore wired to seek out exciting, new situations and environments – to press hard on the gas pedal and propel them onward in their journey. Yet, as Laurence Steinberg (2014) describes, a teenager's braking system takes longer to develop than their gas pedal:

> There is a time lag between the activation of brain systems that excite our emotions and impulses and the maturation of brain systems that allow us to check these feelings and urgings...it's like driving a car with a sensitive gas pedal and bad brakes...
>
> (p. 15)

When the gas pedal and the brakes work well together, an individual knows how and when to be assertive – think of a soccer player accelerating forward to receive a pass – and also when to put on the brakes and pause – think of that same soccer slowing down their pace in order to avoid the risk of being called "off sides." This ability to both accelerate and brake wisely and appropriately is known as "self-regulation" and it is a key variable in successful development. As described by Steinberg (2014), "The capacity for self-regulation is probably the single most important contributor to achievement, mental health, and social success" (p. 16).

Adolescents therefore need lots of practice with both parts of this dialectical skill set: They need opportunities to practice being assertive and actively reaching out for new opportunities. They also need lots of practice thinking before they act and putting the brakes on their assertiveness when they have gone too far. In terms of brain development, this means that their limbic system (akin to an emotional gas pedal) is learning to communicate and work fluidly with their prefrontal cortex (akin to a rational braking system).

Adults can help adolescents develop this centrally important and dialectical skill set of properly navigating the gas pedal and the brakes in a number of ways: First, we can help them understand and have a language for what they are experiencing, telling them about the gas pedal and the brakes, for example. We can therefore help them understand why they struggle with impulse control and the confusing waves of intense emotional highs and lows. We can be sympathetic when they struggle with putting on the brakes. We can help them engage their calming and thoughtful regulatory processes by practicing mindfulness and self-compassion. And, importantly, we can model what it is like to be a self-regulating adult by not losing our own cool when they lose theirs. We can help act as an adolescent's prefrontal cortex – helping with decision-making, planning for the future, and problem-solving. These "executive functions" are exactly what adolescents need to learn from us. We may not feel the same thrill they do from riding a terrifyingly exciting roller-coaster at an amusement park, but we can teach them the deep satisfaction of a calmly composed and well-organized life.

Clearly, adults play a role in helping adolescents develop a good and reliable braking system. As scary as it may sound, we also have a role in helping them to step on the gas pedal. As Steinberg (2014) states:

> The problem is that we want adolescents to take some risks – try out for the school play, take an AP course, run into a scrum of players chasing a soccer ball – but we don't want them to try drugs, break into buildings, or drive through yellow traffic lights.
>
> (p. 75)

Again, paradox: to help our teens make a safe passage through adolescence, we need to help them confront and navigate potentially dangerous situations. The rationale here is based on the fact that we know teens are going to be taking risks, with or without our support, and it is therefore important for us to be involved in which risks they take: Better the devil you know than the one you don't. The following story is from Peter's experience of parenting a fledgling adolescent. It highlights the way we as adult are intimately involved in this adolescent challenge of navigating the gas pedal and brakes:

> My son Noah loves BMX biking. He clearly gets a thrill and a lot of edgy joy from jumping over gaps, racing around steep corners, and dropping over precipitous edges into a concrete skate park. Yikes! One day recently, I had taken Noah to our local indoor bike park where they measure the danger of particular runs and tricks like they do on the ski slopes: green for easy, blue for challenging, and black for dangerous. On this particular day, Noah, who was about 13 years old, pointed at one terrifying "black" ramp and jump in the park and said, "I want to ride that." Noah was pointing at a "gap" jump, in which, if he rode it, he would accelerate up one side of a ramp, leave the ground at maximum velocity, and only return to earth after clearing a gap of about 5 feet in between. Essentially, he would take a short flight at about 10 feet in the air for few seconds. Almost every rational parenting bone in my body wanted to scream out, "There is no way you will ride that! You have got to be kidding me! We are going home now! Pack your things!" Instead, I took a breath to calm myself and said, "Go ask your coach. If he says you are ready, then maybe you can do it." Noah's coach, Levi, thought Noah was ready. Levi had Noah practice a number of times before jumping, and then, amazingly, Noah flew…and landed, safely.
>
> I tell you this story because I think it is a good example of where I had to check my own "braking system" and instead encourage my adolescent's "gas pedal," within reasonable limits. I was truly scared Noah would hurt himself, and he, in fact, has hurt himself on other occasions. But it was important for me to acknowledge and trust Noah's own judgment that he thought he was ready. In this way, I tried to show confidence in his own developing self-understanding, autonomy, and in his own developing ability to self-regulate and make thoughtful choices. It was also important, I think, for me to ask for help from his expert coach, Levi, to see if Levi agreed that Noah was ready for such a jump. In this way, I was not only reassuring myself and assuaging my own fears, I was also showing Noah that it is important to seek expert knowledge and guidance regarding big risk-taking decisions.

This tension in adolescence between the gas pedal and the brakes is not an easy one to navigate. While it is important to allow adolescent risk-taking, there are real dangers for a teen's body and brain if the wrong kinds of risks are taken. As mentioned in the section above on the passage from childhood to adulthood, adolescent brains are in flux: They are literally being reshaped. Unused or redundant neural pathways are being pruned away while more frequently used pathways are being reinforced and strengthened. If an adolescent engages in unhealthy risk-taking and introduces their developing brain to significant amounts of drugs, alcohol, or nicotine, an addictive process in the brain can kick in where greater amounts of those substances are needed to produce the same effect. Adolescents crave the kind of stimulation that comes with such substances, but this kind of overstimulation can reshape the pleasure centers in the brain. As Natterson-Horowitz and Bowers report (2013), practitioners in the still emerging field of adolescent medicine work to keep at bay what they call a "chilling list of threats to young humans," including:

> ...traffic accidents, STDs, alcohol and drug abuse, traumatic injury, teen pregnancy, date rape, depression, and suicide. Much of what we associate with adolescence involves behavioral changes, and lately research has focused on brain changes that help explain those behaviors – like risk taking, sensation seeking, and the somewhat perplexing compulsion to fit in with the group.
>
> (p. 275)

One of the major takeaways for us from our research into the new science of adolescence has been to take seriously a necessary vigilance in protecting our teens, at the same time we are trying to help them "leave the nest" and use their gas pedal in healthy ways. If we used to think that adolescence was time when teens just needed time away from adults to explore and develop, now our thinking has complexified: We as adults need to navigate our own challenging passage between giving space and being present. Another way we have applied our new understanding of adolescence regarding the gas pedal and the brakes has been to create real and exciting challenges for our group participants: We have them navigate an "alligator swamp" as a group in Session 2; we have them make statements about their own likes and dislikes in front of a group of peers in Session 3; we ask them to both give and receive appreciations in the group setting in an exercise we see as a kind of "reverse bullying" in Session 8.

In these ways, we honor an adolescent's need for novelty, excitement, and challenge. We often explicitly frame our group sessions around the notion of challenges to make them more interesting and less anxiety producing (by giving them something external to focus on). Finally, we also implement in our groups many opportunities for students to practice using their braking power in various ways: During the "alligator swamp" activity in Session 2, they are not allowed to speak, but can still find ways to help each other; In Session 5, we work to help them confront a bully in effective ways by role-playing non-violent options; In Sessions 4, 5, and 6, we repeatedly ask them to demonstrate good and respectful listening skills when our group leaders are sharing strategic stories.

In the next section, we take on the third and final challenging passage of adolescence. This passage between affiliation and status is related to addressing what Natterson-Horowitz and Bowers (2013) described above as the teens "somewhat perplexing compulsion to fit in with the group," and is also, as we will show, just another way to talk about how to both "Belong and Be You."

Affiliation & Status

In the first section above, we described how the passage from childhood to adulthood was the answer to the question "*what* is happening in adolescents?" We then detailed how a clear understanding and working knowledge of both the gas pedal and brake is the answer to the question "*how* does this fundamental change happen?" In this section, we identify the answer to the question: "*Why* does this process of profound change occur at all?" In short, we provide this answer by mixing our metaphors: Adolescents leave the nest and use a carefully orchestrated combination of the gas pedal and brakes to navigate developmental challenges – rapids – and develop to become better regulating adults. Why? It's because they need to find a new affiliative group (or groups) to belong to – in addition to hopefully maintaining strong ties to their families of origin. In making these new connections, adolescents also gain a new standing, a new footing, a new status in life, which also allows them to stride confidently into adulthood. As Steinberg (2014) notes:

> One source of not just comfort but basic survival is to identify more with your peers than with your parents…you get companionship on the transitional trek, as well as safety in numbers: Predators will be intimidated by a large group, and you can lose yourself in the group mass. That is one reason why for many but not all teens, fitting in can feel so important – it's an evolutionary holdover of life or death.
>
> (p. 29)

What makes this passage through the adolescent years especially difficult is that teens are not only desperately working to find a tribe in which to belong, to fit in, they are also engaged in the difficult process of finding out who they are as individuals and what makes them unique, what makes them stand out from the group. In this way, adolescents need to learn to join, cooperate and affiliate at the same time they need to discover what makes them unique as individuals. While they are learning to cooperate with others, they also sometimes need to compete in order to differentiate themselves and gain standing and status within their communities. "Get out there and be aggressive," we tell them before an intense game. But we also feel compelled to add: "But not too aggressive!" Clearly there are perils on both sides of this dialectical passage through affiliation and status. We know teens who lose their way in the herd, who lose their own moral compass, their own ability to say both yes and no firmly, risk following that herd into sometimes dangerous territory. We also know that a teen who is never able to connect well with others risks social rejection and the potential traumas of alienation and isolation. Natterson-Horowitz and Bowers (2013) describe the perils of affiliation succinctly:

> Schooling, herding, or flocking – moving within and belonging to a group – gives protection to an individual exiting infancy. A group means more lookouts, more eyeballs, more voices to raise danger alarms. But it comes with a price. Individuals coming together to form a group must learn to be inconspicuous…anything odd or conspicuous makes an animal more obvious to a predator…Perhaps this suggests that before parents condemn a child's desperate plea for the "right" Nikes or jeans as materialistic – or dismiss it as overly conforming – they consider a different perspective.
>
> (p. 292)

To us, this centrally important concern of "belonging" also informs our perspective on the ubiquitous reality and pull toward social media, social networks, and screens that compel the attraction of so many adolescents. Being around peers – even virtually – tends to feels good, and being without them tends to feels bad, as highlighted by Alan Kazdin and Carlo Rotella (2010) in their article *No brakes! Risk and the adolescent brain*:

> Social information (*Are people my age around?*) connects with the brain's processing of rewards—neuroimaging shows that the presence of peers activates the same brain circuitry as does processing of rewarding experiences. Having peers around is a reward, and not having them around is felt as the opposite, which begins to explain your 14-year-old's sullen, moody, heedless demeanor around the house.

Teens need to connect or they risk being painfully adrift. At the same time, as stated by Siegel (2013), being around peers in unsupervised groups is one of the most dangerous settings for adolescents:

> Unfortunately risk behaviors often significantly increase in the company of peers, as demonstrated in experiments that have measured how teens do when driving on a simulated automobile program when alone and with their friends.
>
> (p. 72)

This important and risky need to affiliate underlines the importance for us as adults to make sure that teens get a chance to connect with others in their peer group, while at the same time making sure that we know something about those peer groups, where they are and what they are doing. Too much of a tether is a bad thing, but no tether at all could be even worse. In *A mother's reckoning: Living in the aftermath of tragedy* (one of the most challenging books we have ever read) Sue Klebold (2016) details a heart-breaking account of her regrets of not knowing more about her son Dylan's social world in the period before he became one of the two Columbine shooters:

> I have deep regrets that I wasn't more in tune with Dylan's feelings about the place he spent his days. I wish I had spent much more time and energy on determining the climate and culture of the school…than on assessing it academically.
>
> (p. 91)

Clearly, we need to help our teens find a place in their social systems, and to keep our eye on them as they make those connections. But we also need to help them find their own identity aside from the herd, to find their own standing as an individual. The Latin root of the word status is related to a kind of standing, of station, of stability and clear identity. Status, as described by Faris and Felmlee (2011) is usually thought of as something we shouldn't discuss in polite social settings, but if we are honest, it is as strong a motivator through adolescence as is their need for affiliation. Everyone wants to do well, to be seen as competent, to be held in high esteem. Most of us have dreamed of standing on that awards platform at the Olympics, receiving our medal, or being chosen for a choice part in the big play, or even just being invited to one of the "popular" teen's parties.

As successful adults who have, for the most part, found our own standing in our communities, in our workplaces, even in our sports teams or friendship circles, we may forget what it is like to struggle with finding our footing, with the challenge of discovering who we are and what we are good at. Adolescence is in great part about discovering these wonders, these supports, of our own capacities and strengths. We find that strong capabilities and competencies not only bring us confidence and success, but they also serve as gifts: We are able to share our competencies and successes with others as we enter the generative years of adulthood. We gain knowledge, success, and status in a field of endeavor, and paradoxically that status also provides us with a tribe of like-minded others, of friends, colleagues, and family.

Of course, finding status is as fraught with difficulty as is finding affiliation. The dangers of navigating this passage too far on the side of status are clear from what we can remember of our own teen years: The jocks who thought they were better than anyone else, the socialites who seemed to rule the roost, the "popular" kids who were widely known, but not necessarily nice. How can we help out teens find their own strengths and to use them to better their own lives and the lives of others? How can we help them gain the success and confidence they need to take on further challenges, while also holding a sense of humility and concern in regards to others? These are the questions we hold in our own minds when working with adolescents in our groups.

We ask many of these same questions of them. As stated in the sections above, we find it is helpful to find and share the words and language that describe the actual challenges our teens are facing, to find a language to help them see and understand better their own experience and the challenges they face. In this way, we have found that helping teens understand why wearing the right shoes seems so important can be helpful in giving them a perspective on their own experience. We have found that talking with them about the possible differences between being "popular" and being kind are helpful to them. We have also found that encouraging them to strive for both positive status and positive affiliation gives them a helpful way to understand and direct their own motivations and longings. We help the teens we work with to discover that there are many valid and positive ways of finding both status and affiliation, of finding ways to both belong and be themselves – from sports to music to social clubs to academic pursuits – and that the paths to success, to identity and belonging, are many. As Strauch (2003) relates in her book *The primal teen: What the new discoveries about the teenage brain tell us about our kids*,

> it may also be time to give teenagers a wider definition of what success at this age means, give them more wiggle room to make their own mistakes and come up with their own answers.
>
> (p. 210)

Too often teens are seen as out-of-control, hormonal, trouble-makers. In these sections, we have worked to frame and name the major passages of adolescents: moving from childhood to adulthood, learning to regulate the gas pedal and brakes, and navigating between affiliation and status. In doing so, we hope that both our adult readers and the adolescents they share these concepts with will see the teen years for what they really are: a profound time of change, potential, and risk that requires thoughtful attention and careful navigation. As we have described, there are clear perils as they pass through the risky extremes of each of these passages, these rapids, but there is also a clear sense of success and confidence that comes from finding a healthy line through these changes. As Siegel (2013) describes:

> When we see our emotional spark, our social engagement, our novelty seeking, and our creative explorations as positive and necessary, this period becomes a time of great importance that should not just be survived but nurtured.
>
> (p. 75)

Navigating Adolescence: Five Takeaway Points for Supporting Teens

To summarize this section of understanding and supporting adolescent development, we offer the following "takeaway" points that we hope will be helpful to all group leaders, as well as parents and caretakers who are concerned with the healthy "passage" of the teens in their care:

1 Adolescence is a process of navigating, of charting a way through challenging dialectical poles:
   Between childhood and adolescence, between the gas pedal and the brakes, between status and belonging, and between exploration and focus. Caring adults can help teens navigate adolescence by talking about and naming the journey they are on: The challenges of the move from childhood and adulthood, the difficulties with regulating the gas pedal and the brakes, the struggle to create a healthy balance of status and affiliation, and exploration and focus.
2 Caring adults can help teens navigate adolescence by sharing their own strategic stories: What can you share with them about how you struggled as a teen with risk-taking, with the gas pedal and brakes, with gaining status and affiliation, with both exploring and focusing, and with learning how to be both appropriately assertive and respectful?
3 Caring adults can utilize the "warm yet firm" characteristics of the *authoritative* parenting style (navigating the extremes of overly *permissive* or *authoritarian* parenting styles). Some examples include encouraging independence, placing limits, consequences and expectations on behavior, expressing warmth and nurturance, allowing teens to express opinions, encouraging teens to discuss options, administering fair/consistent discipline, being clear about saying both "Yes" and "No," not sweating the small stuff, or ignoring the big stuff.
4 Caring adults should aim for a 5:1 ratio of positive to negative feedback when interacting with teens in order to establish and maintain a good, working relationship with teens. Examples of positive feedback include showing your affection, care, and concern; giving appreciations; and lightening things up.
5 Importantly: there are many paths through the process...Happy Navigating!

   Navigation/regulation/negotiation
   is a fluid and ongoing process
   of adjustments/corrections/adaptations
   within parameters/boundaries/extremes
   that are established/necessary/containing
   the result of which allows for further
   movement/development/complexity/capacity

References

Faris, R., & Felmlee, D. (2011). Status struggles: Network centrality and gender segrega-tion in same- and cross-gender aggression. *American Sociological Review* 76(1): 48–73.

Goldstein, J.R. (2011). A secular trend toward earlier male sexual maturity: Evidence from shifting ages of male young adult mortality. *PLoS ONE* 6(8): e14826.

Kazdin, A., & Rotella, C. (2010). *No brakes! Risk and the adolescent brain.* Slate, Feb 4, 2010.

Klebold, S. (2016). *A mother's reckoning: Living in the aftermath of tragedy.* Crown Publishers, New York.

Natterson-Horowitz, B., & Bowers, K. (2013). *Zoobiquity: The astonishing connection between human and animal health.* Vintage, New York.

Siegel, D.J. (2013). *Brainstorm: The power and purpose of the teenage brain.* Jeremy P. Tarcher/Penquin, New York.

Steinberg, L. (2014). *Age of opportunity: Lessons from the new science of adolescence.* Mariner Books, New York.

Strauch, B. (2003). *The primal teen: What the new discoveries about the teenage brain tell us about our kids.* Random House, New York.

Part Two

Belong and Be You Group Sessions

A Nine-Week Curriculum: Brief Instructions & Full Descriptions

Overview

In Part Two, we provide a "tried and true" nine-week, social skills curriculum – *Belong and Be You* – that we have designed and modified over the years in our efforts to help adolescents be better socially connected as well as confidently independent. For each week of the curriculum, we first provide brief instructions: a summary and outline of the tasks and materials needed to run the group each session. These brief instructions are best used as a quick reference on the day each session will be facilitated. We also provide a full narrative description of each session based on our experiences over time. These full descriptions are meant to be read in advance of leading the group and provide a richly detailed account and examples of what each session looks and feels like in practice.

DOI: 10.4324/9781003368779-4

Session 1

Opening the Group

Brief Instructions

Overview

Our goals for this first session are to help the participants understand what the group is about, to help them meet each other and the leaders, and to have the students share just a bit about themselves and their own lives. In the "Opening," we introduce a warm-up exercise, describe what the group is about, and ask the students to fill out a "pre-assessment." In the "Body," we have the students introduce themselves and ask questions of each other using the "60-Second Autobiography." In the "Closing," we ask the students to reflect on their experience in the group both verbally (by stating what they liked or learned) and in writing (by filling out the weekly survey).

Materials

- Paper (or Booklets) and Markers, Pre-Assessment, Weekly Survey

Opening

- Welcome participants and lead opening mindful/stretching/calming *Warm-Up* activity:

  "Push your feet into the ground, stretch down and try and touch your toes, roll up and stretch arms overhead, roll shoulders, make faces, wave across the circle, etc."

- Participants add their names and a symbol of a favorite activity to the poster or booklets
- Describe group, goals, norms, and confidentiality:

  "This is a group where we will have fun, feel safe, but also feel challenged..."

- Hand out, read through, and ask participants to complete "pre-assessment"

DOI: 10.4324/9781003368779-5

Body

- Lead *60-Second Autobiography* activity

  "Okay, now we are going to tell our whole life story in just sixty seconds! Impossible right?"

Close

- Ask: "What did you like about today?" "What did we learn about each other today?"
- Describe and read through the weekly surveys and ask them to complete it.

Reminders

- Comment about the shared connections between the members and openness within the group as students shared their unique differences. The drawing and autobiography "game" help group members share about themselves in a fun, indirect way.
- Create clear expectations and norms with the group about participation and respect. Brave spaces happen when children feel welcomed and protected!
- Rely on the structured "turn taking" during the autobiography to regulate their contributions.
- Resistance shows up in different ways. Both high talkers and low talkers might represent healthy anxiety as group members take risks.

Full Description

We hold an image in mind when we think about the overall design of this nine-session curriculum: The shape of a bowl. That is, the first three sessions of the curriculum we consider to be "on the rim of the bowl," and therefore less challenging but important in setting up a sense of safety and belonging. In the second three sessions of the curriculum, the group steps "into the bowl" and uses the support of that container to address more challenging content. In the last three sessions of the group, as we begin to move "out of the bowl" and toward closing, we employ positive and supportive activities to reinforce the student's resilience, hopefully providing them a stronger sense of both themselves as individuals and as group members as they exit. This same metaphor is helpful to keep in mind as the basic structure of each individual session as well. In this way, participants are asked each week to begin with a less challenging opening activity, before "stepping into the bowl" in the body of the session, and mindfully coming "out of the bowl" at the end, transitioning more easily back to class.

To begin this first session of our group, and each session to follow, we lead the group participants through a brief mindfulness, stretching, or relaxation exercise. This simple activity can change every week, or stay the same, depending on the group. Here is an example:

Okay, welcome everyone. Let's warm up a bit: let me see you push your feet into the ground, one at time, like you are pushing through the floor. Good. Now let's stretch down and try and touch your knees and maybe your ankles and maybe even your toes. Nice. Okay, now let's roll up our spine a bit at a time, slowly, and then stretch our arms high over our heads. See if you can touch the ceiling with your left hand. No, try your right hand. Nice effort. Okay, let's drop our arms, and roll shoulders around in circles for few spins in one direction, and then the other direction. Great. Now, let's make a few faces at each other. How about serious with our brows and mouth scrunched up? Great. Now, let's do a crazy face with our tongue hanging out and our eyes cross-eyed. Perfect. Lastly, let's wave across the circle at the person across from us like you haven't seen them in years and they just got here and you are picking them up at the airport. Try both arms because you are so excited to see them! Whew. That's exhausting. Let's take a break and sit down…

Our goals for this first session are to help the participants understand what the group is about, to help them meet each other and the leaders, and to have the students share just a bit about themselves and their own lives. After this quick group stretch, we hand out blank booklets we have made for the students and ask them to write their name on the cover in large, decorative letters. The students are also asked to add a quick drawing or sketch of something they like to do on the cover as well (e.g. a soccer ball, a musical note, a book, etc.). Alternatively, leaders put down a poster-sized piece of butcher paper in the middle of the group and ask the students to draw their symbol around the edges of it instead of the booklets. (These booklets or poster can be used each week for students to continue doodling, making it easier for them to listen and engage.) While the students are working on this, and are quietly engaged and listening, the leader goes over the goals of the group, the expectations for behavior and contributions, and generally works to set a warm and clear tone. We expect that we will have to go over and reinforce the rules and norms of the group each session, so we don't belabor it here, as in the following example:

This is a group where we will have fun, feel safe, but also feel challenged. Each week, we are going to create some challenges for you as a group to accomplish: Some will be physical challenges, some will be social or emotional challenges. We'll have a safe group to discuss the challenges and good things about sixth grade, about making friends, about building community, and about dealing with bullies. How does that sound? The same rules for class exist here: Being respectful, being responsible, making good choices, being safe. Of course, you can talk to others about what the group is about, but let's agree to keep names and specifics private. I do need to note that I will need to talk with other adults if I do hear that someone is planning on hurting another person or themselves. Okay?

As the students are wrapping up their drawings, we let them know we will be talking about what they drew in a minute, but that first we want to have them answer some questions on the pre-assessment form, which we hand out and read over aloud, giving them plenty of time to complete. Once we have collected the pre-assessment, we launch into an activity called the *60-Second Autobiography* with a playful introduction that helps set the tone of the activity:

> Okay, now we are going to tell our whole life story in just sixty seconds! Impossible right? It will go like this: We will go around and start by sharing our name, our symbol drawing, and some things about our lives like if we have any pets, who's in our family, what schools we have attended, where we were born, what languages we might speak, and anything else about our identity we might want to share. We also want you to say a bit about your drawing. I've listed those topics here on this sheet of paper: Pets, People, Places, Preferences, Play, Picture. We will have a time keeper and we will also ask you questions if you have any time left over at the end. This is important: After each person goes, the person on their left will tell us something new that they learned about the speaker and the person on their right will ask a follow-up question. We really have to listen to each other. Got it? Okay, I'll go first to show you what we mean…

After the leader demonstrates the *60-Second Autobiography*, it is the participants' turn. As described in the introduction, we work to hold the balance between supporting and challenging our participants: We want to challenge the participants enough so that they engage and take some healthy risks, but at the same time we don't want to challenge them so much that they withdraw. In this case, the challenge is to speak in a group about their own lives, which is challenging for sure, but for only 60 seconds and with prompts to help them, which is supportive. We have noted over time that if the leader is too concerned about being seen as nice and warm and supportive, they will not challenge the participants enough, as reflected in this example:

Leader:	Okay, so do one of you want to share your pictures and your 60-second autobiographies?
Jackson:	Not me.
Alexia:	I don't.
Pedro:	Nope.
Leader:	Anybody?

In our work, we have found it more helpful for the leader to be directive and specific in their requests of the participants. For example, the leader may say, "Okay, each of you is expected to share in this activity. Who is willing to go first? I'll pick someone if I don't get any volunteers." We have found that students are more willing to share once it is clear that it is an expectation. In this next excerpt from Session 1, the group leader directly asks Tina to say one thing she had learned about Henry, who was sitting next to her and who had just shared his *60-Second Autobiography*. Tina will then be next to share her story.

Leader: What is one thing he shared that you can remember?

Tina: He has a cat named Mister.

Leader: There you go! That was perfect.

Tina: Okay my turn. Are you timing this? Okay, I have three brothers and a sister. I don't have a pet but I live with a pet. My brother has a dog-named Hercules. He's black and white and pretty small. He's four years old. Something I like to do is sleep in or go out with my mom. Languages I speak are Spanish and English. And in the future I want to learn to speak French.

Leader: Oh, awesome! You have time to talk about your picture.

Tina: I drew a picture of me shopping at the mall.

Leader: What store do you like?

Tina: Forever 21, Hollister, and Macys.

Leader: Thank you so much for sharing, that was great. I know it's hard sometimes to speak up, in middle school and even for me now as an adult. I appreciate you sharing.

We have found that many times, the *60-Second Autobiography* is really just about as simple as the one that Tina shared above. That is fine because the goal is just to have the students share a bit about themselves, with a purposeful limitation of just 60 seconds. The impossibility of sharing your whole biography in just 60 seconds is part of the point of the exercise. Interestingly, we have found that even with the very brief amount of time to share, and a set of prompts to respond to, students often have difficulty filling all 60 seconds. In those cases, we make it explicit that others in the group can ask questions of the student sharing until the time is filled. It should also be stated, however, that some students will share quite a bit in the small time allot-ted, and that the leader should be ready for that, as in this next example with Julio:

Leader: Are you ready?

Julio: Um...ok. I have been playing guitar for two years, and I am currently the youngest in my family. My mom is currently pregnant with twins and I, um, am gay and speak two languages too. That's five things right? Is my time up?

Leader: Ha, yes, that's five things. And, no, your time is not up yet. Who has questions for Julio?

Jayda: What two languages?

Julio: English and Spanish...and a little of Korean because I studied it for a month.

Leader: Where did you study Korean?

Julio:	Um, cuz I was in my room and I saw an ad with subtitles in Korean and I was like, "I do not know what it is." Then I watched a Korean anime and I never understood, I always needed the subtitles and I just wanted to learn a little bit.
Leader:	Yeah, that's fun. That sounds really interesting. Thank you for sharing. It is so exciting that your Mom is expecting twins.
Julio:	Yeah, I think it will be two girls, but we don't know yet.
Leader:	Do you have other siblings?
Julio:	Yes, I have a sister that is 23, and I have a brother that lives in Arizona that is 27.
Leader:	Ah. So this will be your chance to be a big brother.
Julio:	I'm an uncle of five.
Leader:	Wow. Well, thank you. I really appreciate you sharing about your identity about being gay, very brave.

At such moments, we hope the leader of the group is able to acknowledge Julio's significant (and risky) sharing, as the leader did in this case, without shining too bright a light on the student or shying away from it altogether. Another balancing act. As mentioned, the goal of this first group session is simply to learn a bit about each other in the group and what is possible in our work together. In this case, Julio has made it clear that real sharing can happen. As reflected in the next two reflections from our group leaders, this idea of encouraging and balancing contributions in the groups are key to their success in reaching our goals of helping the students feel stronger in themselves and more connected with others. One of our leaders, Katie, wrote in her reflective notes after the first session:

> As a leader I hope to address "growing edges" by providing an appropriate amount of challenge to Amina to help her feel more comfortable within our group. During the first group session, Esther was absent so maybe a step towards challenging Amina could be to have her demonstrate the *60-second autobiography* for Esther. As a leader, I have learned that I need to be willing to step outside of my comfort zone and learn to be both comfortable and accepting of silence when it is necessary as well as be comfortable and willing to break the silence when it's needed.

Another of our leaders Nicolette, reflected in her notes on this idea of intentionally helping the students differentiate from one another at the same time they are integrating within the group:

> Reflecting on this first session, especially the process of developing cohesion, certain dialectical skills stand out as especially relevant. First, *integration and differentiation* encompasses the opportunity, especially as presented in the

brief autobiography activity, for students to speak to their own unique personas and lives, while simultaneously becoming more a part of the group: this reflects the relational process by which we become more connected through announcing who we are, and we find out more about who we are through relationship. After experiencing our first group session and debriefing as group leaders, it is apparent that one of our challenges will be to support this process of differentiating while integrating for our student participants who tend to be more quiet.

In the closing activity of Session 1, we ask the participants, just before filling out the weekly survey for the day and returning to class, to share just a bit more, as in the example below:

Leader: So let's just go around and share either something that you liked from today, or something that you're looking forward to in the next few weeks, or both. So I really enjoyed hearing the details that each of you shared about your lives, and I look forward to getting to know you better in the coming weeks. We'll go this way around the circle.

Shanti: I, um, liked that Ashlyn enjoys doing wrestling 'cause, like, I mean, to me wrestling is fun but I don't like to get hurt that much and I'm sensitive.

Leader: It's very brave.

Ashlyn: Um, I enjoyed hearing everyone's, like, hearing everyone speak about their life and getting to know more people in my class because now, um, we'll know each other more.

Tabitha: Um, I think I'm kinda the same as Ashlyn. I enjoyed listening to people's opinions on things 'cause now I feel like I know them better than I guess if I didn't know them before. I don't talk to people as much if I didn't know them that well, so yeah.

Leader: I think lots of people have that experience. Thank you. Yeah, some of us touched on something that's really important in this group, which is just the chance to get to talk to people that we don't usually get the chance to get to know. It's funny sometimes to be in a school with people for so long but not get the chance to connect.

Joining as a Group

Brief Instructions

Overview

The goal of Session 2 is to have the group members gain some experience and trust working together as a group. In the "Opening," we introduce a different warm-up exercise and review the group expectations and norms we set in Session 1. In the "Body," we have the students work together as a group to get through the challenging (and non-verbal) *Alligator Swamp*. In the "Closing," we again ask the students to reflect on their experience in the group both verbally (by stating what they liked or learned) and in writing (by filling out the weekly survey).

Materials

- *Alligator Swamp* Map, Blue "Painter's" Tape, Weekly Surveys

Opening

- Welcome participants and lead opening mindful/stretching/calming *Warm-Up* activity

  "Let's all just take five deep breaths together and on the inhale reach your hands up over your head, and on the exhale, reach all the way down and see if you can touch your toes…"

- Reiterate and emphasize norms regarding making the group both safe and challenging

Body

- Lead *Alligator Swamp* activity at least once (3 × 3 and/or 4 × 4 depending on the group)

  "We have been on an expedition, but we've gotten lost!"

DOI: 10.4324/9781003368779-6

- Process *Alligator Swamp*
  Discuss goals of the activity and solicit responses/reactions regarding their experience:

  "How was it to do this activity?"
  "How was it not to be able to talk? How did you help each other?"
  "How was it to help and be helped?"
  "Not everyone is good at the same thing, that's what makes a group stronger"
  "What did you learn about yourself or others in this activity?"

Closing

- Reinforce norms: "This is a place where we want you to feel included and safe, no teasing."
- Ask each participant to share something they learned in or liked about the group
- Complete weekly surveys

Reminders

- Group members follow your lead and energy level. Prepare and practice the opening and instructions in your own adventurous style. Imaginative play becomes real. The *Alligator Swamp* creates a purposeful space to practice a challenging task.
- Describe and encourage non-verbal assistance within the swamp challenge, reinforcing both seeking and offering help. Asking for help can be hard.
- Open a dialogue to share what was hard/easy about the spatial challenge while noting that upcoming group challenges will provide opportunities for others' strengths to emerge. We all have different strengths and challenges.

Full Description

Keeping this overall metaphor of the bowl in mind, the goal of Session 1 was really to just begin to form a group and have the individuals in that group step forward just a bit to introduce themselves. The goal of Session 2 is to have the group members gain some experience and trust working together as a group to accomplish a somewhat challenging but playful task in the *Alligator Swamp*. We do ask them to begin to "step into the bowl" (or swamp, to mix our metaphors) during this session, but we offer a lot of support for them to do so.

The *Alligator Swamp* is a big hit with most groups we lead. It is fun, but also has its risks. Being playful can be a risk for many students. Developmentally speaking, the students' behavior in groups can reflect both childhood playfulness as well as the keen self-consciousness of adolescence. This self-consciousness can often bring a reticence to be silly, making it difficult to leave behind the "too cool for school" protective stance. As leaders, we help to create a safe and supportive environment for participants by "going there" wholeheartedly ourselves. The *Alligator Swamp* begins with the students standing on one side of a set of Xs that we have placed on the floor about a foot away from each other using blue "painter's tape" in a 4 × 4 matrix, as shown in Figure 2 (leaders can adapt this matrix and create multiple other paths for future use):

Participants line up here

Start

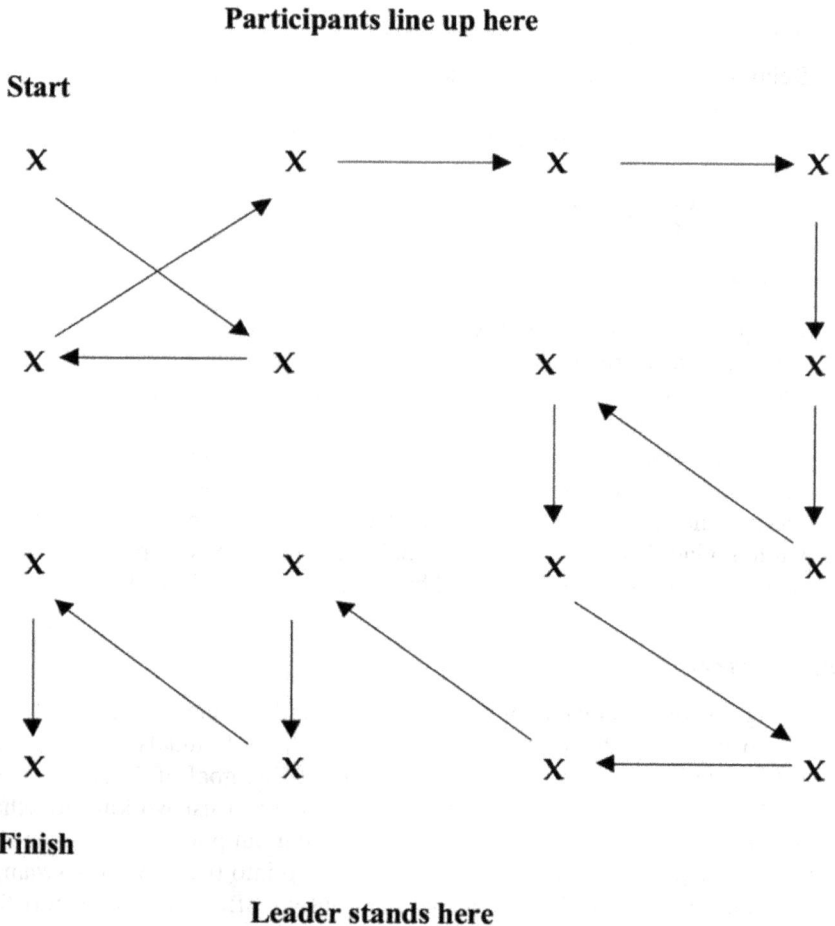

Finish

Leader stands here

Figure 2 Sample Alligator Swamp Path

After participants are set and standing on one side of the "swamp," the leader, standing on the other side, then coaxes the students into an imaginary scenario, with many playful flourishes added, as highlighted in the text below:

Okay, I want you to imagine that we have been on an expedition in 'outdoor school' but we've gotten lost! We've been out for days, surviving by eating slugs and drinking water off of leaves. You each have five bucks in your pocket if we could only find food to buy. We finally get out of the woods and see a store, but it's just on the other side of an alligator swamp! The only way to get across is by stepping on each of the alligator heads without waking them. However, there is a specific path that you must follow to avoid waking the extremely hungry alligators. Learn and memorize the path by watching each other move through it, and you all will make it across safely. If someone steps incorrectly, they must run quickly to the end of the line to avoid being eaten by the wakened gator. You may help each other to remember the path by making hand gestures, but you must remain absolutely silent while your friends are crossing or the gators will wake up. So your goal is to find and walk the path through the alligator swamp silently without waking the alligators. Here are the rules:

1 all alligator heads are stepped on only once in a particular order
2 you will hear a "ding!" when you step on one correctly and you can keep going
3 you will hear a "roar" if you step on one incorrectly, and you have to return to the end of the line
4 each step on the correct path is only one step away from the last, no skipping or leaping
5 you have to do this quietly or you will wake the alligators! Good luck!

During the *Alligator Swamp* activity, leaders offer verbal cues (dings and rawr-rrhs) to let members know if they've made the right choice. They can also offer encouragement and observations about what they are noticing about the group and individual in the group (e.g. "Oh, April is pointing to the next step, that is so helpful!" "Look, Jason is asking for help with his eyes! Who is going to help?"). These observations often reveal to us important information about the current relationships among members, their safety and willingness to ask for help, as well as individual traits of independence and leadership. Once one participant has successfully completed the swamp, that individual receives a big high-five and becomes a helper and guide for the ones to follow. The activity is not over until all members of the group have successfully crossed the swamp, getting as much help and as many passes at it as they need.

Once the activity is completed and the group is basking in the glow of a collective success (which in our experience almost always happens), the leader helps the group unpack the participants' experience within the swamp. The leader conveys explicit messages about the purpose of the group throughout this processing (e.g. "Not everyone is good at everything and memorizing a pattern might be easier for some than others. We are going to be facing all sorts of challenges in the weeks ahead and will need all our talents to make the group work" and also "We wanted to see if this group could help each other through something challenging and we did see that happen!") The leader is also curious about each participant's experience and asks questions about the experience of being helped, asking for help, and offering help. The following is a description from one of our group leaders of a conversation between members after making it through the swamp:

> While all of the group members appeared to enjoy the *Alligator Swamp*, some found the activity more challenging. When posed with the question of what they had noticed or learned about themselves while participating in the activity, one student responded, "I was not very good at it, but I had fun because everyone was helping." Riley, a positive and active participate within the group, was discouraged at times as she struggled with the pattern and was the last person to finish. Despite appearing overwhelmed at some moments, she made it through the swamp with the encouragement and help of her peers and was happy to reach the end. When asked what the purpose of the activity might be, Riley ventured that "it might be teaching other people to be compassionate and helpful towards others." Although Riley struggled through the activity, there was never an instance where another group member teased or became impatient with her. Her peers offered compassion, patience and understanding as they guided her through the swamp. When asked how it felt to be helped throughout the activity, another student, Jason (who is a quiet and reserved group member), replied that, "It felt good." When prompted to elaborate he responded that, "It felt good to be supported." We emphasized how we noticed the support in the group and that it was a good sign that this group could take on more challenges in the weeks to come.

Another example of one of our leaders helping the students process their experience in the *Alligator Swamp* below highlights how no one person can make it through the swamp the first time, requiring help from others:

Leader: How was it when you went and made a mistake? Your team learned from that mistake…What did you notice about that?

Angel: It was easier.

Leader:	It was a lot easier, huh? Rather than going out alone and making the same mistake, somebody else can help you out…
Narim:	I, for one, this is kind of hard for me…so having a team that is able to point when I'm out there, having a teammate pointing, "this one, this one!" I felt much better, much safer in taking the step.
Leader:	I definitely noticed you were really helping each other through. And what did you guys learn about yourselves in going in and working through this?
Maya:	You have to boost your confidence.
Leader:	Yeah! Anybody else?
Willa:	Umm, that sometimes you should trust people.
Abdul:	Teamwork makes the dream work [general laughter and agreement].

Over time, we have found that this playful and challenging game within the second session offers the students a chance to take risks together as both individuals and as a team, coming out of the experience a bit more "together" in their experience. Participants have been provided with enough support and guidance to risk being playful and even make mistakes in front of their peers, therefore building a supportive foundation for their work together in the weeks ahead.

Being Similar and Different

Brief Instructions

Overview

The goals of Session 3 are to have the students say a bit more about themselves as individuals and to recognize and accept the ways they might be both similar to or different from others in the group. In the "Opening," we introduce an *Animal Yoga* warm-up exercise and play a game together called *This or That*. In the "Body," we reintroduce this *60-Second Autobiography*, this time using images of animals on cards. In the "Closing," we again ask the students to reflect on their experience in the group both verbally (by stating what they liked or learned) and in writing (by filling out the weekly survey).

Materials

* *Animal Cards*, Weekly Surveys

Opening

* Lead *Animal Yoga* activity: Eagle, Gorilla, and Lion
* Lead *This or That Animal* activity

   "This is group adventure/challenge where you will get to show your choices about different topics by moving to different spaces along this line...
      Would you choose a cat or a dog for a pet?
      Would you prefer to see animals by visiting the Zoo or out in nature?
      If you were a wild animal, would you live in the mountains or at the beach?
      If you were a wild animal, would you travel in groups or by yourself?"

* Process *This or That Animal*: "What did you notice/like about this activity?"

DOI: 10.4324/9781003368779-7

Body

- Lead *60 Second Animal Cards Autobiography* activity

Step 1: Pick it! "Please pick one or two that for whatever reason catch your attention."

Step 2: Be it! "We are going to go around and pretend that we are the animals we picked."

  - Where do you live, what do you eat, and how do you get food?
  - How do you find shelter and what is your home and habitat like?
  - Do you hang out in large groups, with just a few other animals, or more solo?
  - How do you protect yourself and those important to you and are you generally safe?
  - How are you unique, what makes you special and what cool things can you do?
  - What questions do others have about you?

Step 3: Does it fit? "Now we are going to go around again and say two things."

Step 4: I like it! "Lastly, let's say at least one appreciation to someone else in the group."

Step 5: (Optional if time) Discuss each other's animal cards…

Closing

- Ask each participant to share something they learned in or liked about group
- Complete weekly surveys

Reminders

- Commit to playfully engaging in the animal yoga poses with the group members. Moving the body helps regulate the nervous system.
- Highlight acceptance and understanding when students stand for their preference in "this or that." Being seen as "different" in middle school can feel dangerous.
- Help students describe and "become" their animal before asking them to relate to it. Images can reveal characteristics about ourselves.

Full Description

During the fun and bonding *Alligator Swamp* activity of Session 2, we emphasized the individuals in the group less and the cohesion of the group more. In Session 3, we bring the focus back to the individuals in the group, but indirectly, by first having the participants talk about animals. The goals of Session 3 are to have the students say a bit more about themselves, to step out a bit more, as individuals as well as them recognizing and accepting the ways they might be both similar to or different from others in the group.

We begin with a goofy opening activity based on *Animal Yoga* activities that can easily be found on the Web. Here is an example of how we might begin:

> Okay, welcome to our third week. Let's move our bodies a bit so we can both energize and relax a bit. This is called Animal Yoga, so first I want you to stretch your eagle wings/arms up really high and start flapping like an eagle soaring over the land. Nice. Big slow flaps. What do you see down there on the ground way below you? Okay, nice. Let's land on the ground again and pretend we are a gorilla with big long arms, swinging them from side-to-side, and now stretching them all the way down to maybe touch our toes and make little gorilla grunts. Just hang out in the gorilla stretch for few moments... Nice. Okay, take a deep breath. Last, and maybe most fun, we are going to do the lion pose. Show me your lion claws by extending your hands and flexing your fingers next to your face. Great! Now I want you to add a big lion growl, showing me your teeth and biting down hard a few times. Let's hear that growl! On the last one, stick your tongue out nice and long as you exhale! Nice work with bringing out your animal nature...

This quick opening is a good segue into our next activity which we call the *This or That Animal* activity. To start this activity, have the participants line up on a real or imagined line running across your space and describe the activity like this:

> This is another group adventure/challenge where you will get to show your choices about different topics by moving to different spaces along this line. There is no right or wrong choice, but it might be challenging to notice if you are like your group members or different from them. Remember, our main goals for this group are to have you better understand the ways you are connected to others, as well as distinct from them. We also know that choices are sometimes hard and you might have preferences other than "this or that," so you can choose to remain in the center of the line if you choose both or neither. However, each time we ask you to move at least a little in one direction or another. Okay here we go, I want you to migrate to this end of the line if you prefer dogs, and I want you to migrate to this end of the line if you prefer cats.

After the students have moved to and found their place on the line, the leader makes descriptive observations about what they notice (e.g. "looks like most of you prefer dogs, but there is one cat person over here.") and then begins to ask a series of "unpacking" questions (e.g. "Who could tell me what they like about dogs/cats? What do you like about them?") as well as giving appreciations to those who might have taken a "unique stance" in the activity (e.g. "I really appreciate you, Ashleigh, for having been the only one to take a stand for cats. That takes a lot of bravery, to stand up for what you think is important even when everyone else is going the other way!"). The leader then moves through a series of "this or that" questions with similar follow-up questions as listed below:

Would you choose a cat or a dog for a pet?
   Follow with: What do you like about that pet? What do you not like about the other?
Would you prefer to see animals by visiting the Zoo or out in nature?
   Follow with: What do you like about that location? What do you not like about the other?
If you were a wild animal, would you live in the mountains or at the beach?
   Follow with: What do you like about that environment? Why not the other?
If you were a wild animal, would you travel in groups or by yourself?
   Follow with: What do you like about groups or being alone?

In the transcript example below, the students have chosen a place on the line to show that they like dogs (at one end of the line) or cats (at the other end) and are now discussing their choices, with the leader's help:

Leader:	So you all picked dogs? Why did you pick dogs? What is something you like about them?
Matt:	Um, I like how they are protective of you. I grew up with pit bulls, and they are always protective of you. They are sweet and not really aggressive.
Leader:	Do you have any pit bulls as pets right now?
Matt:	My grandfather breeds them.
Leader:	Do you have a favorite?
Matt:	Her name was Ricky and she was so sweet.
Simone:	I also like them. Like they will be aggressive to other people but nice to you since they grew up with you. Like, German Shepherds are kind of like that.
Leader:	Pit Bulls and German Shepherds are sometimes called aggressive breeds. Do you agree with that? Are they all aggressive?
Matt:	No. They are nice once you get to know them.
Leader:	People can be like that too. They may seem one way at first but when you get to know them…
Matt:	Exactly, like me. I come off as rude sometimes but I am really nice once you get to know me.
Leader:	Thanks for sharing that. I know we are just getting to know you, but I find you nice already.

As this example shows, the unpacking and processing of their choices about dogs or cats can also bring forth more about their own identity in surprising ways. We have found in our work that this kind of "indirect" work (in this case, talking about animals first) can paradoxically lead to very direct expressions of the self. In this next example, one of our groups has returned to the *This or That Animal* activity at the end of the session just for fun and we see once again how direct statements of identity – and in this case cultural identity – can come forth from indirect discussion of food preference:

Leader: Okay everyone! Now I want you guys to either go on this end of the line if you prefer pizza and the other end of the line if you prefer tacos.
              [Leaders and students run to find a spot on the line. Leader stands alone on the pizza only side. Most students are in the middle.]
Leader: Wow! I notice that not many of you like pizza.
Sam: I like pizza but I also like other kinds of foods!
Leader: Anyone from the tacos side want to share why they prefer tacos?
Arno: Well, my family is from Mexico. We make and eat tacos a lot of the time.
Esteban: That's why my family eats tacos often too!

One of our leaders wrote about this activity in their reflective notes for the week, highlighting how lighthearted playfulness in such early activities in the group can lead to more serious discussions:

> Throughout the session, the leaders and the students both engaged in the dialectic of *playfulness and seriousness.* Laughter and fun was ongoing, but everyone also held a sense of seriousness by displaying respect and positively acknowledging differences. Students expressed that being different or standing apart from the crowd can be very difficult in real life and especially with their friends. This lays some serious groundwork for discussions in weeks ahead.

After the *This or That* activity has set a playful tone for discussing identity and differences, the leaders move on to the *60 Second Animal Card Autobiography* activity, which again uses an indirect approach (first pretending you are the animal pictured on the card you have chosen) to lead to more direct and personal statements of identity (e.g. "I'm like an elephant because, well, I like to lead."). In brief, the activity goes like this: For the first step, an array of cards with pictures of animals on them are spread out on the floor in front of the participants. They are asked to sort through them and just pick one or two that they like in particular, for any reason. For the second step, mimicking the structure of the *60-Second Autobiography* from the first week, the participants each pretend they are the animal they have picked, answering the prompts about their life as that animal as they go. For the third step, the participants then reflect on the things they said about their animal and pick one thing (or more) that is also true or fits them in their own life (e.g. "Like this hawk, I tend to be a loner too."), as well as something about their animal that doesn't fit (e.g. "I'm not like this hawk because I really don't like to eat fish."). Steps 4 and 5 are suggestions for processing and extending this activity. All five steps are detailed below:

60 Second Animal Card Autobiography: Five steps

Step 1: Pick it! "Okay, we've spread out a lot of cards with pictures of animals on them. Please pick one or two that for whatever reason catch your attention. Quietly explore all the images and then pick one or two.

Step 2: Be it! "We are going to go around and pretend that we are the animals we picked: just play along with me. Say, 'I am this animal...' and tell us where you live and what its like to live there, what you eat and how you get food, if you tend to hang out in groups or are more solo, if you tend to be aggressive or more quiet, when you sleep and if you are safe, etc. When you are finished, we will also ask you at least one question about yourself as that animal. Here's some prompts for you to tell us your "60-Second Animal Autobiography":

- Where do you live, what do you eat, and how do you get food?
- How do you find shelter and what is your home and habitat like?
- Do you hang out in large groups, with just a few other animals, or more solo?
- How do you protect yourself and those important to you and are you generally safe?
- How are you unique, what makes you special and what cool things can you do?
- What questions do others have about you?

Step 3: Does it fit? "Now we are going to go around again and say two things: The first we want to know if one way in which you are not like the animal you chose in terms of your personality, the way you are here at school, or at home. The second thing we want to hear is one way in which you are like that animal, some way in which you are similar to the way that animal lives, or its habits, or its personality. For example, I'll go first: I picked a jellyfish and a bear. I'm kind of like a jellyfish in that I really like to be quiet out in the middle of nature. I'm okay with hanging out with others like me, but I do appreciate quiet. I also love to be floating and relaxing in the water. I'm not like the jellyfish in that I don't really like to just drift through life. I like to have a plan and to have eyes to see where I am going next. Sometimes I like to be in groups with others, but I also like time to float on my own."

Step 4: I like it! "Lastly, let's say at least one appreciation to someone else in the group for something they shared. Something you liked about what they said, some way in which you have something in common, or just something you didn't know about them before this."

Step 5: (Optional if time) Discuss each others' animals, characteristics you wish you had, some ways in which you want to practice new behaviors or ways of being, or some behaviors you would like to minimalize. Discuss how we could practice such new ways of being here in the group together.

In the following transcribed example of this activity, the students have picked their animal cards (step 1) and already playfully pretended that they were that animal in step 2 (e.g. "I'm an elephant. I'm big and strong and confident..." and, "I'm a tiger, I have a loud growl..."). Now, in step 3, the leaders help them reflect on ways in which they are like that animal they picked and ways in which they are not like that animal.

Jesse: Um, I'm like an elephant because, well, I like to lead, I'm a leader not a follower. And, one way I'm not like elephants is that I don't like to get dirty.

Cassidy: Um, one thing I shared about the tiger was that, sometimes something I do is that I don't know when I'm being really loud, or when I'm being really quiet either. Like people say I'm being really loud or quiet when I think I'm just talking normally.

Leader: I can definitely relate to that. So in some ways, you are kind of like a tiger...yeah.

Crystal: Um, we were talking about the monkey in the card I picked and I said that I want to have a shelter for stray animals, to save the world from testing on animals and keeping them safe from harm.

Leader: So it was probably hard for you to pick just one animal, then. It was really cool to hear your deep connection with the monkey you chose. One of my favorite moments in the whole group was when we were all looking at the images and asking questions to each other. That was really great to have you all participating in that.

While the *Animal Card* activity is helpful in encouraging students to make statements, first indirectly and then more directly, about themselves and their identity in a group setting, it is also helpful as a way for students to have the experience of having been seen and noticed by others, as in the following example:

Leader: One thing I'm wondering, because you all know each other from class, were there any things once you'd seen what your classmates had chosen and heard what they said, where you were like, yeah, you are like that or you are not like that?

Kat: (to Jesse) What Jesse said about being an elephant, I think it's true because she is a leader. She has her own style and doesn't follow what anyone else wears.

Kalea: It's true what Sal said because he likes to do art a lot and he's really good at art. [Sal smiles shyly, not used to being recognized by the popular and vocal Kalea].

As one of our leaders wrote in his reflective note for the week, "This week, we focused on students gaining a stronger sense of self-identity and understanding also how they belong to the group." These are in fact the overarching goals of the entire nine sessions: to help students have a stronger sense of themselves as well as a stronger sense of how they can connect with others. To accomplish these goals in Week 3, we worked through the "indirect" means of the *This or That Animal* activity, as well as the *60 Second Animal Card Autobiography* activity to help the students connect in a more direct way with not only who they are as individuals, but also how they are seen and accepted as part of the group.

In Table 7, we show some of the data we collected after the *60 Second Animal Card Autobiography* activity in Week 3. This figure shows the responses of the 58 sixth graders we worked with that term when responding to the prompt: "When I talked as if I was the animal in my card, the things I said connected to

Table 7 Animal Card Activity Data

Middle School Students (n=58)

"When I talked as if I was the animal in my card, the things I said connected to my own real life."

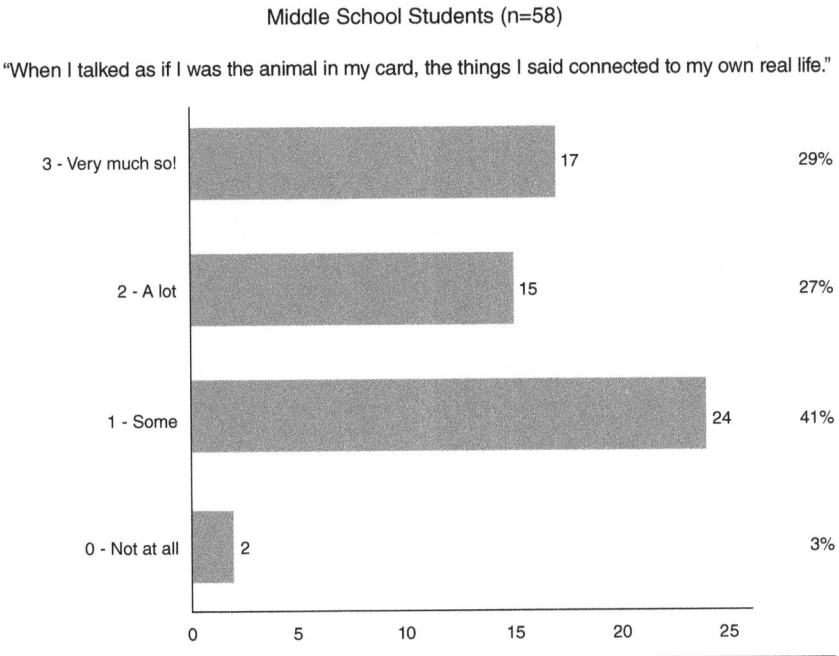

Response	Count	Percent
3 - Very much so!	17	29%
2 - A lot	15	27%
1 - Some	24	41%
0 - Not at all	2	3%

my own real life." The students were asked to circle one of the following options: 0-Not at all, 1-Some, 2-A Lot, 3-Very much so! We were curious to see if the indirect approach of the *Animal Cards* did in fact lead them to more direct personal connections about their own identity. What we found, as reflected in the table, was that 29% of the 59 students responded "3-Very much so!", while 27% responded "2-A Lot," 41% responded "1-Some," and only 2% responded "0-Not at all." Given that 56% of the students responded either "a lot" or "very much so," we consider this activity a success.

In summary, we see Session 3 as an important "bridge" week, not only between the individual students and their fellow group members, but also as a week that sets up success for Weeks 4–7 to come as we more intentionally "step onto the bowl" and in which more challenging content is addressed: We know that individuals who have a strong sense of self and a strong sense of connection with others can more readily take on the challenging topics to follow like managing emotions, addressing bullying and exclusion, as well as finding one's own identity.

Managing Emotions

Brief Instructions

Overview

The goal of Session 4 is to guide the students into activities and dialogue that reflect a bit more risk-taking, but to do so within the supportive container or "bowl" created in the first three groups. In the "Opening," we introduce a check-in exercise called the *Personal Weather Report*. In the "Body," we tell our first "strategic story" based on a theme of "managing emotions." We also read them a picture book based on emotions and discuss it. In the "Closing," we again ask the students to reflect on their experience in group both verbally (by stating what they liked or learned) and in writing (by filling out the weekly survey).

Materials

- Paper for Drawing, Strategic Story on Emotions, Picture Book on Emotions, Weekly Surveys

Opening

- Lead *Personal Weather Report Check-In*

  "You know when they report the weather they show a picture of a few days..."

Body

- Tell strategic story about *Managing Middle School Emotions*
    e.g. belonging, anger, confusion, sadness, etc.
- Process strategic story with group: "What stood out to you from the story?"
- Read/Discuss *The Bear Inside* (or other picture book on emotions)

DOI: 10.4324/9781003368779-8

When preparing to read the book: "I'm curious what you think of this book and the images in it…"

After reading the book: "Tell me one page that stood out to you in some way…"

- Lead *Drawing Your Bear* (or related) activity: Invite participants to draw one or two pictures in their booklets or on a piece of paper.

Closing

- Ask each participant to share something they learned in or liked about group, especially in regard to understanding and managing feelings
- Complete weekly surveys

Reminders

- Help students reflect upon and predict their moods with the weather check-in. Feelings and thoughts are variable.
- Your strategic story will guide discussions about various emotions and responses to them. Narrative is a powerful gateway to self-awareness.
- Overall, the goal of this group is to have them be able to identify, honor, and accept all their emotions and to identify helpful ways they can address those emotions.

Full Description

As the group begins their fourth session together, our intention is to guide them into activities and dialogue that reflect more risk-taking, but to do so within the supportive container or "bowl" created in the first three groups. As described in the opening section of this text regarding adolescent development, the part of the brain responsible for emotional activation (the limbic system) is providing a powerful "gas pedal" while the part of the brain responsible for emotional regulation and good judgment (aka the "braking system") is still developing. We know that the students in our group, therefore, need a lot of practice thinking about the role of emotions in their life and practicing how to respond to them appropriately. We therefore structure this session with three related "indirect" activities: The *Personal Weather Report* allows the students to reflect on their emotions as if they were weather systems. The first strategic story allows the students to hear from an adult leader as they tell a story about working to manage their own emotions as a middle schooler. Lastly, *The Bear Inside* is a children's picture book that uses the metaphor of a bear to help students reflect on their own strong feelings and what to do with them.

Personal Weather Report

The "mindful opening" of the group this week is a bit different from week's past in that we start with a drawing. We ask the students to reflect on their mood (past, present, and predicted) through a weather report check-in. This activity allows the group members to explore moods as changeable and complex as our northwest weather, while playfully likening themselves to a storm of anger or gust of flighty wind:

> You know when they report the weather they show a picture of a few days, with sun, clouds, rain, snow, etc.? That's what we want you to draw in your booklets: three boxes that have yesterday's, today's, and tomorrow's personal weather report. How has the weather been inside you? Have you been feeling stormy with lightning? Have you been feeling a bit foggy? Has it been sunny inside you? What is the forecast? Do you think the weather inside your head will be better or worse tomorrow? Draw it out in pictures then we will share it in the circle to better understand how each of you is doing today.

In Figure 3, one student used her three images to describe how yesterday she felt okay so it was partly cloudy. Today, she said, she felt angry at something that had happened before school, so there was a lightning storm. For tomorrow, she hoped for a better day with pink clouds in the forecast.

Like all the activities this week, the *Personal Weather Report* is an example of the "indirect" style of work that we have described earlier. Through speaking "as if" they are an impersonal weather system, the students will often paradoxically reveal more about their own personal experience than they normally would.

Figure 3 Qualitative Data Example 1 – Personal Weather Report

Strategic Story: Managing Emotions

Next, the group leader tells the first of four strategic stories that will scaffold the conversations around emotions, friendships, bullying, belonging, and uniqueness in the upcoming weeks. The story told in this session centers around managing challenging emotions in middle school. We use the word strategic intentionally, in that the stories are mined thoughtfully from the leaders' personal experience and polished to create an engaging narrative that begins with descriptive details, introduces a type of "trouble" or challenge, and ends with a purposeful reflection about why the story is being told. For more information on how to remember and construct such strategic stories from your own experience, please refer Part One of this book. Part Three of this text also supplies examples of strategic stories for this and other topics.

We prepare the group and set norms for safety as the leader tells this story, knowing the students who share after will be offered the same reception of respect:

Leader: So I'm going to tell a story about when I was in sixth grade, when I was your age. Do we all think we're ready to listen to the story?
Group: Yep, mmm-hmm.
Leader: Perfect, because this is kind of hard for me to tell so I want to make sure that we're all being properly respectful. I know you guys are all capable of this so I'm not worried.

An example of a compelling strategic story regarding the difficulty of managing middle school emotions is provided below, a real-life example from one of our leader's own experience:

When I was in the sixth grade, I went on a weekend trip to the beach with my best friend and her parents. My friend and I spent hours out in the sun, swimming in the ocean, surfing the waves, and practicing cartwheels on the beach. Everything was perfect until we were getting ready to go home and I noticed my skin hurt. I looked down and was shocked to see I was bright red from head to toe. I had forgotten to apply sunscreen and was sunburnt really badly. It was painful, but I shrugged it off and hopped in the car. After all, I had had my fair share of sunburns in the past, and figured it would probably fade away by the time I went back to school.

When I woke up for school on Monday morning, I looked into my bathroom mirror to find that the sunburned skin on my face had not faded as I hoped, but instead had turned a deep reddish-brown and was starting to peel. Panicking, I picked at the flakes of sunburnt skin and peeled them from my face. Unfortunately, this only seemed to worsen my problem, and soon my face was splotched and speckled with patches of dark sunburnt skin and light pink new skin: a mosaic of ugliness, right there on my face for everyone to see. I was horrified. I wanted more than anything to stay home from school and hide my face, but knew this wouldn't fly with my parents. Maybe it wouldn't look so bad in real life. Maybe people wouldn't notice. Either way, I was forced to take my chances. I reluctantly hopped on my bike and rode to school.

I made it through my morning classes without anyone saying anything about my face. Then lunchtime came. As I walked into the crowded cafeteria, I felt curious glances come my way. I tried to tune out the looks from my peers as I walked to the table where my friend group was sitting, and pulled up a chair. I watched my friends react, their eyes widening, their mouths gaping, some of them catching themselves and averting their eyes, others asking the question that seemed to be on everyone's mind: "Your face...What happened?"

"I got sunburned," I murmured. "And it's peeling." I sat there quietly, wishing I was invisible. My friends took turns making remarks about my face, saying they had never seen such a bad sunburn. They also tried to reassure me, saying it would go away soon. Yet, the damage was done, and my embarrassment escalated. Right then, Cindy, a friend from my after school ballet class, was walking by our table when she saw me and stopped.

"Whoa, Monique. What happened to your face? You look like you have a disease!" She chuckled. My face turned hot and my eyes began to well with tears. I couldn't hold it in anymore. I slipped away from our table and darted for the girl's bathroom, where I broke down crying. I was so overwhelmed with embarrassment and shame about my face, and even anger at my friends for noticing my sunburn and myself for forgetting to wear sunscreen in the first place. I wanted to hide away forever and never show my face again. Shortly after, my friend Liz came into the bathroom to comfort me. She didn't say anything, but just hugged me, waited with me, and listened to me while I cried and told her about how terrible that day was. I still felt embarrassed, but having Liz listen to me made me feel less alone, and that helped me get through the rest of the day.

The reason I am telling you this story is because sometimes things may happen that feel so embarrassing that you'll think you'll never get past them. These moments are really tough. The good news is, eventually, that moment will pass, and some day, it won't feel like such a big deal. When you find yourself in a place where your emotions are overwhelming, remember it's ok to feel that way, and that you don't have to go through it alone. Honor your feelings, and don't be afraid to find comfort and understanding in a friend, family member, or teacher.

It is common for group members to truly melt into this "story-time," eyes fixed on the leader, mouths widening at dramatic moments within the leader's reflection. We believe this happens for a couple of reasons; one, they are ready for the content to deepen and for things to become "real." Additionally, there is a healthy disclosure offered by the leaders that allows the leaders to be seen as fallible humans too. Group members often feel empathetic toward and protective of their group leaders as they hear these real-life stories.

After the leader tells the story, the co-leader helps the group to make sense of what they heard and possibly make connections to their own lives. We encourage the leaders to begin this reflection by asking members, "What did you notice about the story?" or "What stood out to you from this story?" These questions are in contrast to more pointed and direct questions like: "Have you ever felt like that?" or "Has that ever happened to you?" which we have found tend to shut the discussion down by being too direct. Like the *60 Second Animal Card Autobiography* activity from last week, we have found that children will share more about their own experience, directly, if we ask them about it indirectly. In this case, when we can get the students to highlight what stood out to them in the leader's story, it often leads to more personal and direct contact with their own life experience. Other helpful prompts during the processing of the strategic stories include, "What ideas do you have about how the leader responded to the situation in their story?" or "Can you relate to any of the emotions the leader was feeling?" and "How would you have responded?" The intention of these deeper conversations isn't to create absolute answers or best responses, rather to honor the complexity and challenge of managing emotions and to create a safe place to explore multiple options for healthy responses.

The Bear Inside

After the story about managing middle school emotions has been presented and discussed, the group leader reads aloud an illustrated book written by Peter Mortola and Mark Molchan called *The Bear Inside* (2016) (This book can be found in multiple languages on YouTube). Alternatively, a different picture book can be used in place of *The Bear Inside*. Suggestions include *Ahn's Anger* (2009) by Gail Silver and Christianne Kromer and *My Monster and Me* (2021) by Nadiya Hussain.

We do tell the students we work with that this book was written for younger kids, but we are curious what they think about it. The book explores a child's experience with managing strong feelings such as anger and aggression. The language and illustrations in the book highlight examples of a child's emotional experiences dealing with siblings, with bullies, and with their own "inner bear." When our leaders process the book after the reading, they ask the students which pages stood out to them. As in the "indirect to direct" examples from the processing of the strategic stories above, the students will often begin talking about their own experience by first highlighting what stood out to them from the book. Usually, in this way, the big themes in the book end up being talked about anyway, such as how to regulate anger and aggression that is directed either outwardly or toward the self. In the illustration below (Figure 4, The Bear Gets Mad) of one particular page of "the bear inside", the bear turns on the child after striking out in baseball.

In the following excerpt from one of our group discussions, the leaders help the students explore how aggression can turn inward (after striking out in baseball, for example) and how to quiet that inner aggression and quiet those negative self-statements by challenging one's own inner critic.

Leader: So, I wanted to ask you all if there were certain pages in the book that stood out to you. Maybe you liked it, or you had a question about it. I'm going to ask you each to name a page. What comes to mind, Ross?

Ross: Why is the bear small in the picture? [points to the "points to the image in Figure 5 Wrestling with the Bear," below]

Leader: Oh, right, why is he small in the picture? And he's really big here, right? [previous page]

Ross: Mm-hmm

Leader: The bear is breathing down your neck and telling you you're no good. And then you're wrestling the bear, and he's gotten so small.

Ross: I know. Why is he so small?

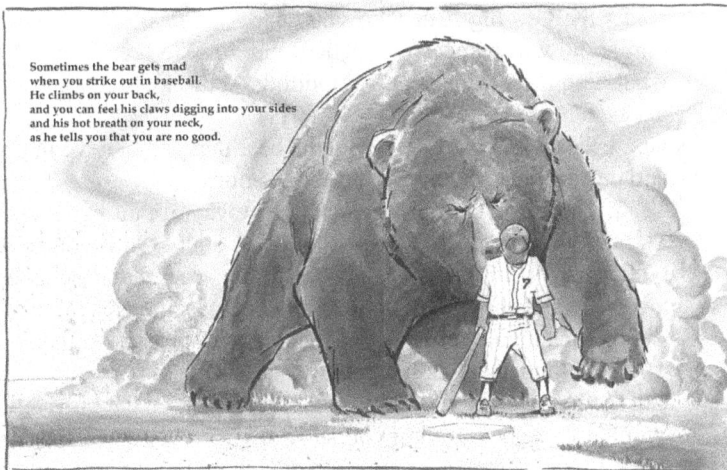

Sometimes the bear gets mad
when you strike out in baseball.
He climbs on your back,
and you can feel his claws digging into your sides
and his hot breath on your neck,
as he tells you that you are no good.

Figure 4 The Bear Gets Mad

But you have to wrestle with that bear,
and put him in his place.
You need to teach him to be respectful of you and others.
You have to be just as tough as that bear.

Figure 5 Wrestling with the Bear

Leader:	He's small! Why do you think he's small? Why do you think he was so big and now he's so small?
Heidi:	Because he's a teddy bear.
Leader:	Because he's a teddy bear. What I was noticing is that this bear came out and he's big and he's making you feel like you're no good, it just feels so big. But then you tackle the bear, you wrestle with him so he will respect you better, and now he feels small…That's what I noticed. Alex, you're nodding. Why do you think the bear gets smaller?
Alex:	Um, because the kid is showing the bear that you believe in yourself and he can't tell you you're not good enough.
Leader:	Yeah! That's really great! That's a great way of putting it.
Jade:	The kid with the bear. He has a lot of emotions, so if you're feeling really mad, I think the bear is really big. And when he's happy it looks like he's having fun and so the bear is smaller.
Leader:	That's such a good observation. Thank you for sharing that.
Maddy:	The bear kinda sounds like a bully.
Sincere:	But the bear is inside of you, so wouldn't you be the bully?
Wan Li:	Wouldn't you be bullying yourself?
Melissa:	Well, it kinda happens, right? When you are feeling bad and you tell yourself that you messed up?
Maddy:	How are you supposed to be friends with yourself?

Sincere: I'm friends with myself.

The Bear Inside also offers scenarios when aggressive feelings and actions might be helpful in protecting oneself and others. As one student notes in the following conversation, the bear can be an advocate, standing against bullying:

Leader: Claire, do you have a favorite page in the book?
Claire: Probably. Like the one where the bear's fending off against the bullies.
Leader: Right, here it is [Figure 6 The Bear Can Help You When You Need Him]. What was it about that page that stood out to you?
Claire: Um, like how he's like defending off the bullies and not just taking it in, actually standing against them and doing something!
Leader: Yeah! He's not just taking it. He's being active. He's standing up for himself!
Natya: Yeah!
Leader: Right. Have you ever had your bear do that for you?
Natya: [quietly] Mm-hmm.
Leader: Mm. What do you think, Diego?
Diego: Uh, it's his inner beast. Someone who backs you up if something's happening that's bad.
Leader: Mm, so someone that backs you up. Something that is always there to help you.
Diego: Your bodyguard.

Figure 6 The Bear can Help You When You Need Him

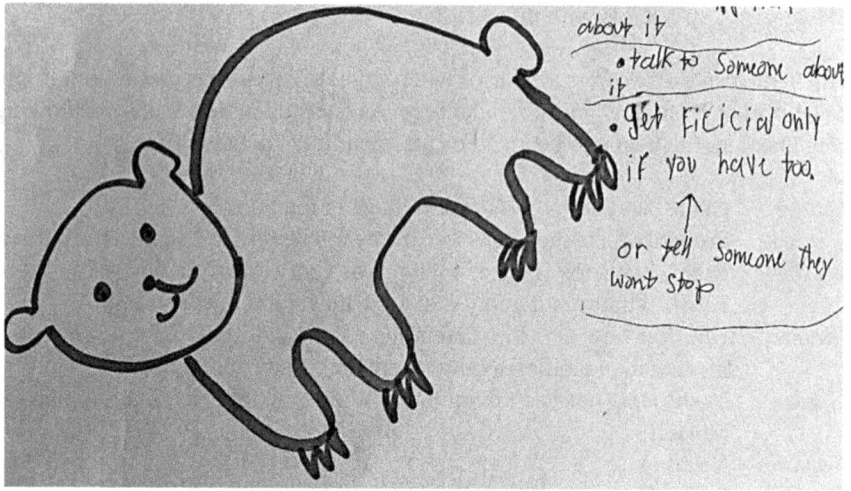

Figure 7 Qualitative Data Example 2 – Drawing of a Bear

Leader: Yeah, like your own personal bodyguard. I really like how you guys emphasized it's always there, it can help you…So maybe even if it is being released, and that anger or frustration is coming out, maybe that's helpful for you to realize and know about it.

In addition to discussing their reactions to *The Bear Inside*, to wrap up this activity, we invite participants to draw an image of their own inner bear. Specifically, we suggest that they draw one or two pictures in their booklets and we give them the following prompts: (1) a picture of their own bear in a challenging emotional situation; and/or, (2) a picture of a way in which they soothe/manage/take care of themselves when they are experiencing strong and difficult emotions (e.g. perhaps by talking to a friend or family member, engaging in exercise, taking ten breaths, taking a break, talking nicely to themselves, etc.). In the example in Figure 7, one student drew a picture of a bear and reminded themselves in writing what they can do when faced with bullying: confront them about it; talk to someone about it; get physical only if you have to; or tell someone else they won't stop.

Through the *Personal Weather Report*, the leader's own strategic story on managing emotions, and the reading of *The Bear Inside*, we have been exploring this week's complex emotions and emotional situations and ways to manage them. As one leader reflected on Session 4:

The students connected taming your bear to believing in yourself. Your bear can at times make you feel less than, and it is important to reinforce feelings of self-worth. I think these insights connect directly to the goals of our group.

Students often feel a sense of relief and connection to others when they hear that their leaders and other students in the group may have struggled with challenging emotions as much as they have. In "stepping into the bowl" of emotions during Week 4, we have set the stage for even deeper emotionally-related content next week in Session 5 when we will confront bullying as a topic, as well as the myriad of emotions that bullying evokes for them in their lives.

References

Hussain, N. (2021). *My monster and me*. Penguin Random House, New York.

Mortola, P., & Molchan, M. (2016). *The bear inside*. 19th Avenue Press, Portland, OR.

Silver, G., & Kromer, C. (2009). *Ahn's anger*. Plum Blossom Books, Berkeley, CA.

Addressing Bullying

Brief Instructions

Overview

Our goal in Session 5 is to leverage the cohesion – the support – that has been building over the previous weeks in the group to now address the risky and challenging content regarding bullying in a meaningful way. In the "Opening," we introduce a warm-up exercise called the *Rainstorm* In the "Body," we tell our second "strategic story" based on a theme of "bullying." We also have the students anonymously list the ways in which they see bullying happening in their lives. In the "Closing," we again ask the students to reflect on their experience in the group both verbally (by stating what they liked or learned) and in writing (by filling out the weekly survey).

Materials

- Strips of Paper, Strategic Story: Addressing Bullying, Poster Sized Paper, Weekly Surveys

Opening

- Lead *Rainstorm* activity: "Can you hear the sound of the rain beginning to fall?"

Body

- Tell strategic story about bullying (e.g. direct, indirect, bystander, etc.)
- Lead *Snowballs About Bullying* activity:
    "You each have three strips of paper: (1) On one strip of paper, write down the top three things that you see students get bullied for (e.g. race, class, ability, gender conformity, physical characteristics, family, religion, ethnicity, age, etc.). (2) On the second strip, write down the top three places students get

DOI: 10.4324/9781003368779-9

bullied (e.g. school hallways, after school, on the bus, on social media, etc.). (3) On the last strip, write down the top three reasons why bullying is so hard to stop. When you are finished, crumple up the strips of paper and toss them into the center. One at a time, each of you will pick one up and read it aloud we will create lists on this big paper."

- Lead discussion based on lists and identify themes
- Discuss both helpful and unhelpful responses to bullying
  - e.g. unhelpful = silence (internalizing) or aggression (externalizing)
  - e.g. helpful = recognize, refuse, report; stop/walk/talk, etc.
- Discuss "snitches get stiches" and what we can/should share with others
- Co-leaders & students role-play new behaviors/responses to bullying situations

Closing

- Ask "How can we support each other in these bullying situations like we do in this group?"
- Ask each participant to share something they learned in or liked about group
- Complete weekly surveys

Reminders

- Continue to include mindful embodied openings and closings each session. The structure and consistency of the curriculum help to build safety for vulnerable content.
- Highlight power dynamics and the fluid roles we embody in both your stories and the contributions of members. Bullying is more complex than victims and perpetrators.
- Encourage students to "try on" different voices in the role-playing using examples from your story and theirs. Reenactments and role-playing help to practice empowered behaviors.

Full Description

In Session 5, we are now "diving into the bowl" with some of the most challenging content we will address in this group: What students get bullied for inside and outside of school and what they can do about it in response. Our goal for this session is to leverage the cohesion – the support – that has been building over the previous weeks in the group to now address this risky and challenging content in a meaningful way. We don't want to just repeat to them what they have already heard about bullying: We know that most students receive three-step lessons in which they are told that they should (1) ask the bully to stop, (2) walk away from the bully, and (3) report it to a responsible adult. We know these recommendations are helpful, but only to a certain extent.

We have found that middle school students benefit from discussing the issues related to bullying at a deeper level in which we can address difficult questions like: What do students get bullied for? What if it is your friend who is the bully? How do you make repairs if you have been the bully? How are relational aggression and bullying related? What if the bullying gets worse if I walk away from it? Our hope is that the students leave this session feeling more supported and less alone because we have surfaced and been willing to talk about some of the real complexities about this issue of bullying. This helps in part simply because the students appreciate us addressing their real lived experience and not glossing it over. We also think it helps the students better understand bullying, why others (and sometimes we ourselves) engage in it, and what they can do about it in response. It may be no surprise at this point, but we assert that the two most helpful protective factors in relation to bullying are found in the title of this book: Belong and be you. As we have stated, the overall goals of this book are: to increase the student's sense of belonging and connectedness as well as increase their strong and independent sense of self. Specifically in regards to bullying, after this session, we want the students to feel less alone in their experience and more connected in their possible supportive networks. We also want them to begin to find their own voice in order to resist and push back in helpful ways when they are aggressed upon.

In this session, we begin with an energizing opening exercise called the *Rainstorm* before we move into a strategic story regarding bullying that the leader shares. We then dive into an activity called *Snowballs About Bullying* and close with a role-playing activity in which students try out different scenarios to resist bullying.

When the students are standing in a circle, ready to start the group, the leader offers this prompt to begin the *Rainstorm* opening activity:

Okay, welcome back for our fifth session together. We are going to warm up with an exercise called the *Rainstorm* so please follow my actions: Can you hear the sound of the rain beginning to fall? [rubbing hands together for a few moments]. Oh wow, the drops are coming down heavier now! [Snapping fingers for a few moments]. Oh my gosh, it's really pouring! [slapping thighs for few moments]. Look at the big thundercloud up there, do you hear the thunder? [hand claps and foot stomps for few moments]. Thank goodness that cloud is passing and it's just back to heavy rains [slapping thighs], and even that is lightening up [finger snaps] and maybe now it looks like the rainstorm is passing altogether [rubbing hands lightly] and all that's left is the wind [blowing sounds] and now its calm. Nice. Okay, today we are going to be talking about the storms we face with bullying and we are going to start with a story that I brought to share with you…

The telling of this particular strategic story about bullying is a difficult task for leaders. The content of this strategic story tends to bring up some of the most traumatizing aspects of their own middle school experience for the adult group leaders. Therefore, the stories are carefully worked on and worked through before they are told to the children in order to make sure the content is processed sufficiently so as to not breach personal or professional boundaries in the group counseling context. Despite the difficulty, we have found that our group leaders are willing to share such difficult stories because they know they are doing important service for the children: they are using their own pain for the student's gain. One consistent theme that has emerged over the years in these groups is how students are bullied and teased for some aspect of their physical self, the way they look, the color of their skin, the clothes they wear (or can't afford), the size of their body, etc. Here is one of our group leader's strategic stories on this topic as an example:

I have a story to share with you about a time I was bullied by a couple of my best friends. It is kind of personal and I really need to know you will be respectful as I tell it. Thumbs up if you can do that. Okay, great. Here we go. Well, as I said, this is a story about a time I was bullied by a couple of my best friends. Well, I thought they were my best friends. It was in the summer going into sixth grade. My two best friends, Stella and Kira, were really powerful friends. They were outgoing, funny, and always had friends around them wherever they went in school. They would tease others with really clever words and always had a snarky come-back for anyone who challenged them. At the end of sixth grade, I was starting to get into a little more conflict with them and they were becoming closer friends with each other as I was drifting apart from them.

During that summer, I went on vacation with my family for two weeks and when I came back, there were 27 messages on the answering machine. I had just gotten my own phone line and answering machine because my mom thought I was using the main house phone talking to friends too much of the time. I was really surprised to see 27 messages, because I was used to seeing just one message every few days from a friend. 27 was a lot! I was excited and almost nervous to push "play," but I did, and I what I heard was Stella and Kira for the next 27 messages. The first message was,

"Oh my god, you're so ugly, it's hilarious that you don't have any friends. Nobody likes you. Katie doesn't like you, Nita doesn't like you, Teri doesn't like you. They all told us they hate you. You're such a loser! *click*."

The next message was, "Your face is so disgusting, 'Points.' "[They used to call me 'points' when they teased me about my nose, but I never thought it was that funny.]" You have huge bug eyes that are so bulging and ugly and your feet might as well be skis, they're so huge and gross. Oh, and you're flat as a board, too. Even the boys think you're ugly. Goodbye, ugly-face *click*."

The next messages continued in the same way and Stella and Kira would mix in animal noises, belches, long periods of silence and then call me a "f-ing B" again and again and again.

Around message number 13, I burst into tears and started crying really hard, kind of yell-crying, but I couldn't stop the tape, I had to keep listening. As I was crying, my heart felt like it had exploded, because my chest was hurting and hot. Stella's and Kira's words really got to me and I believed everything they said, because they both were closer to everyone in our friends group than I was. I was afraid they were telling the truth about how no one liked me. I'd also shared some of my insecurities about my body with them and they were using those things I told them to now make me feel even worse about myself. It was so hard to hear and I started to really hate myself and really believe that everyone hated me.

My mom heard me crying in my room downstairs and came down to check on me. She came in and asked what was wrong and I told her about these messages that were still playing. She started listening to them with me and I remember her reacting with silent anger and head-shaking. She turned the answering machine off and hugged me.

I asked my mom for help. She contacted Stella's mom and Stella ended up writing me an apology letter. I also saw a counselor, which ended up being really helpful. What I wish I'd done, though, is not give them the power to get to me the way they did. They wanted to hurt me, and I basically gave them the permission to do that by taking them seriously.

The reason I'm telling you this story is that I know what it's like to be bullied and to feel betrayed by friends and I'm sure some of you have experienced something similar. Friendships can be really hard to figure out in middle school. I also had other friends who dropped me without giving me a reason, then they wanted to be friends again after a time. Even Stella wanted to be friends with me again after a while. It was all confusing and emotionally hard. I want to emphasize that it really helped asking for help. My mom was really understanding and supportive of me, and still is, while Stella and Kira didn't stay important in my life for very long. It was also really helpful to see a counselor after this: She helped me see how I didn't have to let those girls' opinions be so important. I gained confidence in my own understanding of what made me a good person. I want that for each of you as well.

As you can imagine, this story had quite an impact on the students. This tough example of "frenemies" set them all up nicely to share examples from their own experience in the next activity called the *Snowballs About Bullying* in which they are asked to list three things that students get bullied for. After they write these examples on small pieces of paper, they are asked to aggressively crumple them up, and throw them into the center of the group (symbolically crushing and throwing away these painful experiences). When everyone is done with this, each member takes a turn picking one snowball and reading it aloud while the leaders make lists of the types of things students get bullied or teased for. It is very important that the students who write on any given snowball are allowed to stay anonymous. We ensure this as best we can by having them all write in pencil, as opposed to colored pens, and by telling the students they may not be guessing aloud who wrote what. After hearing and listing all the challenging things written on the "snowballs," a discussion follows, as in the example below:

Lana: It's kind of sad.
Leader: It *is* kind of sad.
Alexia: There are so many reasons and none of them are good.
Lana: Like, someone judges you for, like, how you look, and you can't really control how you look. Everyone looks different.
Alexia: We're all beautiful in our own way.
Leader: That's right. So, let's look at our top answers so we can really understand this. The top thing students got bullied for was looks. After that it was clothes. Race was the other top issue that we get bullied for. Regarding where we get bullied, the places listed most often were at recess or on the track. The lunchroom was also listed.
Alexia: It's basically at school. Everywhere at school.
Leader: What I didn't hear was the classroom which is good...
Alexia: Yeah, because there are teachers in the classroom.
Leader: Yeah, it's a supervised environment. The unsupervised parts of school seem less safe.

In this discussion, the students learn that they are not alone in being teased or bullied for their looks or race, for example. They also learn that while unsupervised areas of the campus can be unsafe, their classroom can be a safer place. These are all good things to be aware of as a student. Here is another example from a different group of where the discussion can go after the "snowball" activity:

Leader: Which ones do you think are the most common? [Referring to the snowballs]
Emily: The clothes? [other students nod their heads]
Leader: Who has ever been teased for their clothes or appearance?
Miguel: It happens a lot, like if you wear Sketchers®.
Latisha: I love Sketchers®, I think they are comfortable.
Leader: Who decides what is cool or uncool?
Latisha: I'll tell you. See Jordans®? (Latisha pointing to Jay's shoes.) How they are like stylish. Sketchers® like light up and people say that they are like childish. Has to be Jordans® or Nikes® or Adidas® or Tims® or Concordes®.

Ariana: I bet if all of the other kids wore Sketchers® then they would be cool.

Leader: Yeah that is a good idea, what would happen if everyone started wearing Sketchers®?

Latisha: Then everyone would think they were cool. Now that we are talking about this I need to say something. I used to be a bully. There were kids I didn't like and I would say they were ugly or they couldn't afford this or that. I would feel bad when I got home. When I got to sixth grade I would see people get in fights or bully and I stopped bullying because I didn't want to do that anymore.

Leader: Thank you for sharing that Latisha. I can look back at times where there were things that I did that was bullying behavior, but it might not have felt that way because there were others doing it too. It's something when you look back you feel bad about.

Owning one's previous ill-advised behavior is the first step to changing that behavior. In this instance Latisha has not only owned her previous bullying behavior, she has done so in a group of peers who have now heard her and still welcome her. One of our leaders commented on this instance in his reflective writing on the session:

> This felt like a big moment for our group. Latisha had become comfortable enough in the group that she felt she could divulge information about her own past and bullying behavior. This reminded me of the dialectical skills integration and differentiation. She put herself at risk for speaking out about her own embarrassing experience (differentiation), but then she was embraced by the group for sharing her experience (integration). I don't believe that it is a coincidence that Latisha shared about her own past of being a bully after the rest of the group was willing to be vulnerable regarding their past experiences as well. Latisha saw that there was support in the group and I believe she felt safe enough to talk about something she was not proud of.

Discussions of bullying tend to be quite animated, which often serves as a good segue into the role-playing activity that comes next. Because clothing and looks were a top category for bullying in one of our groups, the leaders stood up and improvised a skit in which they worked with the group to come up with an answer to one student's experience with bullying:

Leader 1:   [dripping sarcasm and speaking to Leader 2, who is wearing a boldly striped black and white top,] Nice top! What are you trying to do, look like a zebra? I guess that's cool if you want to be a Zebra. Whatever…

Leader 2:	[looking to the sixth-graders] Ouch! What should I say back to her?
Lana:	Maybe you could just say to her, "I don't love all your clothes, either"
Leader 2:	How can I respond without just insulting her in return though?
Natalie:	[a normally very quiet student] Yeah, you could say, "I bet you have some clothes that not everybody likes, too. I gotta go. I'm gonna go find my friends."

We have found that the role-playing activity is one of our student's favorites. They have told us it is fun to see the leaders take on these roles, but we also suspect that they feel empowered by being given a safe and supportive opportunity to practice confronting a bully, to practice coming up with actual words that are so hard to find in the moment. Our group leaders often struggle with the same issue, as we all do. We ask our leaders to record and listen to sessions and reflect on what they learned. Here is a set of comments from one group leader to close this chapter on what they are learning and what they want to improve for the weeks to come:

The work I have to do is practice asking insightful questions to students that might prompt them to reflect and share more. These skills fit the immediacy and structure dialectic. After Alexia and Lana said there was bullying and teasing "everywhere at school," I would have liked to ask how students navigate those unsupervised places. For example, do they avoid going to the bathroom if someone is already in there? Do they take different routes to avoid certain people who are unsafe? What are strategies they use, or they have seen others use when they are teased? What works or does not work? Talking openly about those common experiences would have created even more familiarity and connections among them. I also noticed, hearing the recording of the session, that I transitioned quickly into the Snowball activity after my strategic story. I now question this rapid shift I made as the facilitator. Thinking back and knowing I shared the painful and complex emotions I faced as an eighth grader in my story, I believe I felt timid about taking a pause to reflect with the sixth grade students. I am now aware that after telling my story to our students, I felt I would be taking an emotional risk in asking for their questions or comments. What if they thought my story did not apply to them or asked me about one of the more hurtful verbal attacks made to me by my bullies in the story? Would I be able to explain it without fumbling? Perhaps I could have asked, "What did you notice about my story? What stood out for you? Did you hear things in that story that you related to? Which parts? What do you think you would have done in that situation? Do you have any questions about the story or was there anything that was confusing?" In closing, this was an eye-opening session for me. The role-play activity as an exchange between two of the facilitators took the pressure off the students to comment on their own examples of teasing or being teased and created a collaborative environment where even the most reluctant student was able to participate. Second, I discovered the immense value of recording and listening to group sessions as a learning exercise. Being able to replay each section, take notes, and identify opportunities for improvement will undoubtedly help me become a much more experienced group facilitator more quickly than through practice alone. Through audio review of my strategic story I also found an unexpected confidence in my voice as I shared one of my most trying personal stories and learned that there are opportunities for this story to become a launching point for students to share their own challenging stories, helping them create their own coping strategies for future encounters.

Exploring Belonging

Brief Instructions

Overview

The goal of our sixth session is to center on the issue of belonging and the ways in which our participation within social groups impacts our lives. In the "Opening," we introduce a mindful exercise called "connecting through kindness." In the "Body," we tell our third strategic story, this one focused on the week's theme of belonging, and we also have the students draw representations of their own experiences in places where they experience a sense of belonging. In the "Closing," we again ask the students to reflect on their experience in the group both verbally (by stating what they liked or learned) and in writing (by filling out the weekly survey).

Material

• Strategic Story, Drawing Materials, Weekly Surveys

Opening

• Lead *Mindfulness* activity: *Connecting Through Kindness*

"Let's close our eyes, wiggle our toes, feel our weight on the ground, empty out our lungs, and then a take a big breath in..."

Body

Introduce *Belonging Story* with prompt:

"Over the next two weeks we are going to explore both belonging and being unique..."

DOI: 10.4324/9781003368779-10

- Tell strategic story about the challenges and benefits of belonging to a community, discuss
- Lead students in creating their "belonging drawing" using the following prompt:
  "We just heard a story about belonging, and now I'd like you to think about all the ways that you belong..."

- Have each member share their own drawings and have group ask follow-up questions
- Discuss the benefits of belonging (acceptance, safety, support) and then also discuss the challenges of belonging (needing to conform, social pressures, losing your own voice)

Closing

- Give appreciations for having not teased but rather supported each other in these discussions, ask students to say one thing they liked about today
- Complete weekly surveys

Reminders

- Use the "kindness" opening to help shape thoughts toward positive experiences. We can influence our mood with our thoughts.
- Highlight the risks and benefits of belonging through your strategic story and conversations with group members. Belonging is a developmental drive for adolescents.
- Work with their drawings to highlight multiple contexts, places, and groups in which they can belong. Indirect work can help students explore experiences.

Full Description

Our sixth session centers on the issue of belonging and the ways in which our participation within social groups impacts our lives. This issue of belonging is especially relevant to the adolescent population we work with as identity and affiliation become prominent developmental needs as we described in the introductory section of this curriculum. This session is composed of three parts: (1) an opening mindful exercise called *Connecting Through Kindness* (with an additional, optional warm-up trust exercise in which students have the opportunity to practice trusting others and experience connection through a physical challenge); (2) listening and responding to a group leader's carefully crafted strategic story about belonging; and (3) drawing representations of their own experiences in places where they experience a sense of belonging.

Connecting Through Kindness

As with our opening exercises in the previous weeks, this week's mindfulness activity is meant to help the students "arrive" in the group, experiencing themselves in the moment, taking a few breaths, and then contemplating how kindness helps us connect and feel connected to others:

> Let's close our eyes, wiggle our toes, feel our weight on the ground, empty out our lungs, and then take a big breath in...Hold it, let all that good oxygen get absorbed in your lungs, and turn into energy for our muscles, all the way out to our fingertips. Now let your breath out in a rush! All that carbon dioxide that you don't need, but will feed the trees outside...One more time, big breath in...hold it...then let it out. Okay, with our eyes closed, we are going to contemplate kindness. I'd like you to think of something kind that you have done for someone. Maybe you helped someone in your family with something at home, or you helped a friend, or someone you don't even know, at school. Notice how it made you feel doing something kind for someone else. Now, I'd like you to think about something kind that someone else did for you, either here at school, or at home, or somewhere else. Notice how it made you feel to do something kind. Lastly, think about something kind you could still do today for someone who might need it, a kind word, a kind deed, or just saying hi. Sharing kindness with others is one way to show how you belong with others, how you are connected. So today we are going to talk about belonging. When you are ready you can open your eyes...

Trust Lean (Optional)

Depending on your own group and situation, you may want to include this *Trust Lean* exercise, which dramatically helps the students feel a sense of support and connection. The *Trust Lean* is a slightly less risky version of the classic "trust fall" that most of us are familiar with. The group offers a safe place to "fall" within what we call a "trust lean" challenge. To begin, the group leaders assess (and continually assess) the safety of this task, knowing it is a true physical risk that might be hurtful. The leaders ask the students to create a semi-circle around a student and to put their hands up in a "ready to catch" posture. Students then practice "catching" one of the leaders as he or she leans back toward them, careful to have at least two pairs of hands on the one who is "falling." While the leader first demonstrates being caught after leaning backward for just about six inches or so, gradually the length of the lean/fall is increased to about a foot or more so there is a real sense of letting go and a sense of trust in those who will catch you. Important verbal prompts by the one who will lean ("ready to fall") and those who catch ("ready to catch") are used each time this attempted. Obviously, with this exercise, there needs to be particular attention given to issues and concerns involving touch as well as body awareness and spatial comfort levels.

Students are given a chance to "opt out" of the experience as well as a chance to share concerns and participate in creating measures that help the group feel safe. When we have run this activity, it is usually the case that not all the members of the group participate.

Leader:	Amalia, what was it like to fall?
Amalia:	Uh, it wasn't that scary
Leader:	It wasn't that scary? You felt like you could trust them? Felt supported? Everyone, how did it feel to be supporting Amalia when she was falling?
Kevin:	Good

Other exploratory questions include: "How did you know it was safe?" "What messages were you receiving that it felt safe?" "What was hard about supporting someone who was falling?" As in previous weeks, group leaders take time to reflect on the experience with group members, encouraging and highlighting our inherent goal of trusting the group to take risks, and more importantly, being able to discern what is trustworthy.

Strategic Story: Belonging

After the opening, one of the group leaders introduces the strategic story with the following prompt:

> Over the next two weeks we are going to explore both belonging and being unique. Both belonging and being unique are super important in order to do well in life, but they also have challenges as well as benefits: It's not helpful to belong so much that you lose yourself in the crowd, and it's also not helpful to be so unique that you are completely disconnected from others. Today we will explore both the strengths and challenges of belonging and we'll start with a story.

One of the leaders then shares a story about their experience of belonging to a group. We encourage leaders to complexify the issues of belonging, how belonging is necessary and important but can also be problematic. We ask leaders to note both the benefits of belonging (e.g. sharing common values and experiences, gaining a sense of safety, etc.) while also noting some of the possible challenges that come with belonging (e.g. going along with a group that is participating in dangerous activities, becoming overly conforming, losing one's sense of uniqueness, etc.). As one leader reflected about the topic of this particular strategic story:

> My journey is one in which I experienced many inadequacies, mistakes, and painful situations, and it's one that a lot of students will, unfortunately, find

relatable. Self-compassion was a critical development in my healing, and without it, I would not be able to rise to the challenges of life (like finding out where you belong).

Here is an example of a strategic story regarding the challenges of finding a place to belong. This story could also have been used as an example of a strategic story on "being unique," a topic we address in the next session. In that way, it shows who both "belonging" and "being you" are related. More examples of such strategic stories can be found in Part Three of this book:

Okay friends, I get to tell you another important story about when I was younger. Last time I told you about a time when I had to manage some confusing and difficult emotions but this time I'm going to talk about finding how I belonged. Spoiler alert! It took awhile. So we are going back in time, to when I was in fourth grade. Alright, little me, nine-years-old, and feeling weird as ever. I'm sitting in Mr. Tunnel's class, looking at some cool lizard specimens he had brought in for our science lesson. I'm having a grand old time until I look at the clock. "Oh dang," I think, "It's gonna be recess soon..." I felt my stomach start to do that thing where it's trying to summersault out of my throat. Then I think, "Will someone want to play with me today?"

I leave the safety of my favorite teacher's classroom, walk out into the hall to get my coat and start the solo journey out to the recess yard. I can feel the wind on my face as my class-mates rush pass me to join their friends. I didn't really have that option. We had this split in our school and in our class: There were the "popular" kids and there were those that were not. There were kids who had a ton of social power, and there were kids who did not. There were kids who were wanted by their peers, and there were those who were not. Looking out into the yard, you could immediately see who belonged to each group.

Many of the kids in my class knew how to be popular, powerful, and wanted. I tried my best to create a me that people would like, just like them. I picked the most popular kids and analyzed them. I tried to figure out exactly what made them likable and I tried to be like that. I told my mom where we needed to shop, I paid attention to what they said and tried to copy it. I bet you guys can take a guess as to how well that went, huh? Yeah, that stuff did not work at all. I think all my classmates could tell I was trying to wear a pretend suit that just didn't fit.

In middle school, I had one friend. One person that didn't make me want to put on that pretend suit. And she was great! Reyna! You remember her from last week? I finally had someone that would stand up for me when people pointed out what was wrong with my outfit or my laugh. I finally had someone that liked my outfits, and my laugh. I felt what it was like to belong to someone else, and to have each other's backs.

But then the summer before eighth grade, Reyna had to move. Now she was going to a new middle school and a different high school too! I was so scared because now I had to go back into the lion's den of middle school without my battle companion. I also knew that at the end of the year I would be going into the even BIGGER lion's den of high school with nothing but my awkward and uncomfortable self. I felt like I was going to be eaten alive. Now I flash forward a bit: It's my first day of high school. My dad had just dropped me off, and taken his embarrassing "first day of school" photo, and now I'm walking into the school in what I hope is my best outfit (it was not – layered tank tops were very "in" back then). Then, the next thing I know, I'm in Mr. Sweeny's first period social studies class sitting next to the girl that was about to change my world.

Her name was Yesi, and she was the COOLEST person I had ever met. She was totally unlike any of the others kids that surrounded me. She was 100% herself, 100% of the time. She was funny, she was kind, and she was loyal. She immediately made me feel comfortable, and as I watched her interact with the world, safely, just as she was, I started to see that there was room for me to do it too.

As I started to feel comfortable, this web of community started to grow around me. I never really belonged to a "group" in high school because I never quite fit into any of the available boxes or cliques. But people did voluntarily walk into my life and ended up staying. By allowing myself to just be who I was, I invited others to do the same as well. We started to belong to each other as "weirdos," as just ourselves, trying our best. The reason I'm telling you this story is that I realize now, until that year when I met Yesi, I didn't really feel like I even belonged to myself. Learning about myself, and knowing who I was, helped me find the kind of people I belonged to, and helped me belong to my own self. So I hope you can take away from my story how important it is to know who you each are as individuals, to belong to yourself first, so that you can also find others who you can belong to. Thanks for listening.

When asked what they noticed about the Leader's story, the students begin to explore the implicit and explicit norms of popularity and what it is really like to belong:

Will: I noticed that it was divided into the people who were popular and the people who were not and I don't think that's cool. People are sad that they don't have any friends and then the popular people just brag about it.

Leader: It's interesting to me: I think that some people who might appear popular, like they have a lot of friends, might still feel alone too because they are not really being themselves. It's like a lot of us are feeling lonely together, but not talking about it, and that can make us feel even more isolated.

Leah: Something I noticed was that it wasn't just like that in sixth grade, but all throughout elementary and middle school. That can be, like, really tough trying to figure out who you are because you feel like you should be a certain way, but that's not who you are and yet you don't know who you really are.

Avia: It was kind of good that you were different because then you can make friends with people who are popular and not popular. Like they can become friends because they are nice, because who cares whose popular and not popular, it doesn't matter.

Belonging Drawing

During the last segment of this sixth session, students are prompted to draw some representation of belonging. They are told by the leaders that it can be, for example, a picture of themselves within a group inside or outside of school, in their family, or as part of a community organization, a team they might belong to, a club, etc. They are told they can draw symbols and colors to represent the group if that is preferred over a literal representation. This can take some of the pressure of being a "good artist." Here is an example of the prompt for the belonging drawing:

> We just heard a story about belonging, and now I'd like you to think about all the ways that you belong: Belonging with a group of friends in your neighborhood or school, with your family, with a church, with a sports team, or a club you belong to, a special class or hobby you go to after school, whatever. I'd like you to choose one situation in which you feel a sense of belonging. Hopefully, you feel safe there, you feel like you can be yourself, and you feel accepted and supported. But you may have other feelings about belonging too, and we can talk about those too. Now I'd like you to take a few minutes to quietly make a drawing showing how you belong. It doesn't have to be a good drawing, it could even just be colors, lines or shapes and you can tell us what it represents. Let's take a few minutes to do this drawing of you belonging...

After they are finished, the students then share their drawings with the group and how it represents something about belonging. In the following example, two students describe unique ways of connecting, of belonging, and ways in which they don't feel connected:

Laron: In my drawing, I'm playing basketball with my friends and we share the love of sports and like hanging out. I don't feel like I belong

	sometimes because I joke around, and they don't. If I do joke, then they don't laugh at it.
Leader:	So there are parts of you that make you feel like you can connect with them, and other parts that make you feel like you don't connect with them as much. I think that's pretty normal.
Tomas:	This picture is when I was in sixth grade. We each have our own PlayStation™. Now that we actually have to focus in school and things are getting harder, we all just play together when we need a break.
Leader:	So you don't even have to be in the same place to feel connected to them! That's really cool. Especially when they live across town or something like that.

In the next example, issues of culture and playful aggression are described. Jay provides an example of how groups can set up norms that make the group distinct, and, although rough looking from the outside, perhaps paradoxically safe:

| Jay: | My group is at lunch. It's a Russian group, but you don't have to be Russian. We don't kick anyone out. We don't care, we just like to have fun arguing. We don't argue in a rude way. We argue in a way that we can laugh too. Like if we make up a joke, then we can argue about it. We give each other a hard time when we tell a joke, and we all laugh. We swing at each other, but in a good way. That's my group. |

Our central goal for this sixth group is to provide multiple opportunities to think and talk about belonging, through experience, narrative, and drawing. The following conversation encapsulates the overarching goal of both feeling connected to others, while also being able to feel strong and safe to be yourself:

Leader:	What is helpful about being part of a group, feeling like you belong with a group of people?
Rowan:	Feeling like you have people that can support you, so if something bad happens, you know exactly who can protect you.
Leader:	So, feeling more confident, you have some protection, you have some help.
Bishu:	Someone I can trust on.
Leader:	Trust. Carmen, what do you think is a good part of being part of a group?
Riley:	You can be yourself.
Leader:	That's a great one!

We intentionally explore themes of belonging in Session 6 before we explore what makes us unique in Session 7. As the title of this curriculum states, the main developmental goals for teens are to find both a strong sense of "belonging" as well as "being you." We have found that grounding our students first in a sense of community in Session 6 allows them to more freely explore the ways in which they are unique as individuals in Session 7. Before we leave this section, we'd like to share an eye-opening and unusual example from a recent group that made us think about this sense of belonging in more complex ways. This past spring, in one group, there were two different students who, when asked to do their "belonging" drawing as described above, chose to draw themselves alone, one on the beach and one in the forest. One of these students, when asked to talk about their drawing, said simply: "I feel most like I belong at the beach." This basic but quite profound statement made us reconsider our emphasis on having to belong to others (e.g. friends, family, communities) as opposed to the experience of feeling a profound sense of belonging in nature, for example, or with our pets, or just simply with ourselves. From this point forward, we will be sure to add such options in the prompt for the belonging drawing.

Session 7

Being Unique

Brief Instructions

Overview

The goal of our seventh session is to focus on strengthening the self of the individuals in the group. Specifically, this means helping them identify and "own" what makes them unique. In the "Opening," we introduce a mindful exercise called *Tense and Release*. In the "Body," we revisit the *This or That* game with new prompts that help them differentiate from each other. We also tell our fourth strategic story, this one focused on the week's theme of being unique, and have a discussion about the benefits and challenges of being unique. In the "Closing," we again ask the students to reflect on their experience in the group both verbally (by stating what they liked or learned) and in writing (by filling out the weekly survey).

Materials

- Strategic Story, Weekly Surveys

Opening

- Lead *Mindfulness* activity: *Tense and Release*
  "Let's stand up and take a big breath in, and as you do, tense your leg muscles for 5 seconds
      Tense them hard but not to the point of pain or cramping. Now breathe out, and suddenly and completely relax your legs (don't relax them gradually). Relax for 10 seconds."

Body

- Lead *This or That Revisited* activity with this prompt:

DOI: 10.4324/9781003368779-11

"Remember when we played *This or That* a few weeks ago? Well, this is a variation on that activity…"

- Would you rather read a book or play video games?
- Do you prefer breakfast or dinner?
- On a weekend, would you rather be inside or outside?
- In school, do you prefer math or reading?
- Would you rather have a one good friend, or lots of friends?
- When you feel anger do you share it with someone or do you prefer to keep it to yourself?
- When you feel sadness do you share it with someone or do you prefer to keep it to yourself?
- Do you find it easier to belong, or to be unique?
- Process *This or That Revisited*: What did you notice/like about this activity? What did you learn about a group member that surprised you?

- Tell strategic story about the challenges and benefits of being unique or different and lead discussion with students responding to this prompt: "Something that makes me unique & special in terms of school, interests, family, friends, race, culture, identity, gender, etc. is…" Discuss differences, uniqueness, identity, and acceptance in our community

Closing

- Give appreciations for having not teased but rather supported each other in these discussions, ask students to say one thing they liked about today
- Remind participants that there are two more sessions of the group and complete weekly surveys

Reminders

- Lead *Tense and Release* to create a foundation to discuss uniqueness. Grounding the body connects to emotional regulation.
- Spend time during *This or That* to explore how and what students do with big emotions and the helpfulness/challenges of each emotion. We can learn from how others deal with big emotions.
- Continue to maintain a brave space with expectations of group members' attention and respect. Making "I Statements" about what makes them special strengthens the self.

Full Description

In Week 7, with just a few weeks left before the group closes, our goals, as they have been from the beginning, are to focus on strengthening the self of the individuals in the group while at the same time to increase their experience of belonging and feeling connected to others as well. These goals are particularly important as we enter the final phase of our sessions with the children: We want to make sure they take from the group a strong sense of self and a sense of connection to others that will support them even after the group has ended.

We begin with another mindfulness activity which gives them an opportunity to feel grounded in their own bodies and experience before we take on the challenges of the day. This one is called *Tense and Release* (which provides students with an opportunity to practice a physical manifestation of a dialectical "range of motion"):

> Let's stand up and take a big breath in, and as you do, tense your leg muscles for 5 seconds. Tense them hard but not to the point of pain or cramping. Now breathe out, and suddenly and completely relax your legs (don't relax them gradually). Relax for 10 seconds. Okay, Let's take another big breath in, and as you do, tense your back and arm muscles for 5 seconds. Hold it, then relax for 10 seconds. Okay, Let's take one more big breath in, and as you do, tense your face and neck muscles for 5 seconds. Hold it, and relax for 10 seconds. Now notice the difference between how your muscles feel when they were tense and how they feel now that they are relaxed. You can do this anytime: When you have a very tense muscle, you can practice tensing and relaxing that muscle area without going through the whole routine. Now just notice for a moment how solidly you can stand on your own two feet, how you have a place to stand, and how it feels good to take up that space. Today we are going to be talking about how we can confidently stand on our two feet, how we can be ourselves, how we can be the special and unique person we are, and how we can receive appreciations from others for what makes us unique.

After the opening, we return to a favorite activity, with a twist. In Session 3 of this curriculum,, you will remember, we led the groups through the activity called *This or That* in which they were asked to take a stand somewhere on a line/continuum between choices such as "Would you choose a dog or a cat for a pet?" or "If you were a wild animal would you travel in group or by yourself?" The purpose of this activity in Session 3 was to help the children begin to differentiate from others in the group by making fairly simple choices and discussing them aloud in the group.

In Session 7, we return to the *This or That* activity with new questions and a more focused goal of having them "take a stand" as an individual within the group based on more challenging criteria. As detailed in the prompt below, the questions this week, like in Week 2, are simpler at the start. After a few warm-up questions, we raise the level of challenge with tougher questions. Here is the complete prompt:

> Remember when we played *This or That* a few weeks ago? Well, this is a variation on that activity. Remember, there is no right or wrong choice and it still might be challenging to notice if you are like your group members or different from them. We also know that choices are sometimes hard and you might have other preferences than "this or that", so you can choose to remain in the center if you choose both or neither. But each time we ask you to move at least a little in one direction or another. Let's get started!

- Would you rather read a book or play video games?
- Do you prefer breakfast or dinner?
- On a weekend, would you rather be inside or outside?
- In school, do you prefer math or reading?
- Would you rather have a one good friend, or lots of friends?
- When you feel anger do you share it with someone or do you prefer to keep it to yourself?
- When you feel sadness do you share it with someone or do you prefer to keep it to yourself?
- Do you find it easier to belong, or to be unique?

These questions get the group discussing their similarities and differences in a deeper and more hopefully more supportive way: They are able to state their preferences and idiosyncrasies, what makes them different from others, while still being accepted and included in the whole group. Our goal with the more challenging questions is to highlight that each approach (e.g. keeping feelings to self versus sharing them with others) have benefits as well as challenges (e.g. keeping feelings to yourself at first may actually be helpful because it allows some reflection and thoughtfulness about who and when to share them). Our leaders make it a point to ask each group member to say one thing about their choices during this activity, such as, "Amy, can you say more about why you prefer one friend to being in a group of friends?" and "Jonah, what is it about keeping your strong feelings to yourself that is helpful?" We do this because we are challenging them a bit to speak their own truth, based on all the support we have been providing them over the past seven weeks.

After the *This or That Revisited* activity, one of our leaders shares another prepared strategic story with the focus of that story being "uniqueness" and both the benefits of and struggles with being unique. One of our leaders, Noah, shared the following story in his group:

> When I was in middle school, I didn't think I was particularly good at anything. I wasn't the best athlete. That was Kevin Killy. I wanted to be the best

athlete. I wanted to able to throw the football farthest and best, but I couldn't. I wasn't the smartest kid in my class either. That was Lynn Hubble or Mimi Letski. They were good in math in a way that I knew I never would be. I also wasn't the most popular kid in my class. That was probably Nick Charboneau. He had big parties that I sometimes was invited to and a sometimes wasn't.

When I was 11, I started playing baseball on a little league team. I struck out so often, other boys used to taunt me by standing around the backstop and yelling "strike out king!" every time I got up to the plate. But when I turned twelve, suddenly I could hit the ball really well. I remember our first practice that year when I was swinging and making contact and wondering, "How am I doing this?" That year I became an all-star, for the first and only time. I'll say more about that in a minute.

When I was also about 12, my middle school teacher announced that there was going to be a speech tournament at the high school that we could sign up for. I don't remember why, but I did sign up. We had to write and present our own speech in front of a whole classroom of people. I remember being nervous, but I felt pretty good about my speech and I actually came home with a bronze speech medal that I still have to this day, still attached to my key ring!

The reason I am telling you this story is because I think finding out about what makes you unique takes a bit of work and a bit of discovery. I discovered I was good at baseball when I was twelve and before that I thought I wasn't. Finding out what makes us unique also takes some time and it may in fact surprise us. I didn't even know that being good at speech was a thing! And little did I know that I would be using that skill throughout my life: I'm a counselor now and it is a really important part of my job to write well and speak well. Also, when I was 11, the most important thing to me was to be a great athlete. By the time I was twelve, I was a much better athlete, but even though sports are still a nice part of my life now, it is less important to me. Whereas, being able to speak well in front of groups like you about important things like how each of us is unique is super important to me now. So I think it's important to give yourself some time and be open to discovering and maybe being surprised about what you are good at, about what makes you unique, and about what skills you have that will develop into life-long strengths.

Our groups have taken different approaches to help students discuss their own uniqueness after a strategic story such as the one above is told. Some leaders have had their groups make "uniqueness shields" on which they draw four images of different aspects of themselves (e.g. culture/family/skills/hobbies) and then share them with the group. Other leaders have chosen to hand out a drawing of an outline of a tree with branches and roots. The students draw or write examples on these tree outlines of what supportive "roots" help them "bloom" in particular and unique ways in their own lives.

The theme from the story above regarding how sometimes it takes a bit of discovery and surprise to find what makes one unique is emphasized within the following group transcript example below. In addition, this example also highlights how sometimes we need to be connected to others before we can discover ourselves.

Leader 1: Let's go around the circle and everyone share one thing that makes you unique! I will model it. First I will say, "Something that makes me unique is …" and then I will say it. So, something that makes me unique is that I like bowling and I will eat anything.

Bruno: So you would eat old pickles?

Leader 1: I actually ate old pickles yesterday. They were barely expired and tasted just fine.

Leader 2: [laughs] That is unique. Thank you for sharing.

Nico: I am unique because I am really encouraging to people. Like I encourage people to do something they might not think they are good at.

Leader 2: It's important to be a supportive person. Right on.
[Rebecca had a difficult time answering the prompts so we told her that she could have some extra thinking time and we would come back to her.

Joel: I am helping and caring.

Leader 2: Those are really important qualities. Those are good ones.

Blake: I have a really big family. There are around 500 people in just three generations.

Leader 1: That is really amazing.
[We then went back Rebecca who was having a hard time coming up with how she was unique.]

Rebecca: I am unique because… Umm….

Leader 1: I have one for you if you need some help [Rebecca nods]. I have noticed that you always make the coolest and most creative fuzzy stick creations during our group with those materials we bring each week.

Leader 2: That's true.

Leader 1: You are always building and designing things every week. You always make something new. I really appreciate that about you. That's an important thing to think about. It is sometimes hard to think about why we are unique. Sometimes other people can notice something you might not have considered before.

Rebecca: So, I guess, I am creative!

Session 8

Giving and Receiving Appreciations

Brief Instructions

Overview

The goal of our eighth session is for each sixth grader to practice the equally challenging skills of both being able to receive compliments from and give compliments to their fellow group members, building on the trust that has developed over the past seven weeks. In the "Opening," we introduce a mindful exercise called *Grove of Trees*. In the "Body," we first teach what good complements look like before setting up an activity in which every student receives compliments not only from the leaders but also from every student in the group. In the "Closing," we ask the students what it was like to both give and receive compliments as well as again asking them to reflect on their experience in the group both verbally (by stating what they liked or learned) and in writing (by filling out the weekly survey).

Materials

- Prepared appreciations for each student, Weekly Surveys, Blank cards for each student on which to write appreciations

Opening

- Lead *Grove of Trees* activity
   "Let's all circle up for this activity. Imagine that you are a tree, firmly rooted in the earth…"

Body

- Lead *Appreciations* activity (recording each response for use next week):

DOI: 10.4324/9781003368779-12

"We've learned a lot about each other these past 8 weeks! And one thing we can give each other to help support each other is simply appreciations..."

"There are different kinds and levels of appreciations..."

"Between each person we will do a little game to unwind..."

Closing

- Lead *Reflecting on Appreciations* activity:

    "What was it like to receive appreciations?
    "What surprised you?"
    "Which appreciation have you not heard about you before?"

- Remind participants that next week is the last meeting
- Complete weekly surveys

Reminders

- Highlight the strong roots of individual trees and the collective power when connected as you lead The Grove of Trees. The group activity represents individual and collective strength.
- Protect this space with fierceness and clear expectations for participation. Receiving appreciations requires vulnerability and trust.
- Make time to model how to give an appreciation and offer time to prepare appreciations for each other, brainstorming positive adjectives, and maybe writing them down. Connecting feelings to language is often challenging.

Full Description

Often the greatest rewards come with great risks. Over the previous seven weeks, our group leaders have guided the sixth graders through experiences of multiple activities and conversations to develop both vulnerability and trust among them. They have now arrived at a pivotal session in which this trust will be tested and reinforced. During this first of two closing meetings to round out time with the sixthgraders, the students are asked to notice and speak directly to their classmates, giving them compliments and noting their strengths as group members. In addition to giving compliments, each sixth grader will also practice the equally challenging skill of being able to receive compliments from their fellow group members.

The Grove of Trees

As in previous weeks, we open with an activity representative of the challenge ahead. The grove of trees is an adaption of the "tree pose" in many yoga practices.

We guide them in a mindful description of what it feels like to be grounded, deeply rooted, with branches that grow and stretch in many directions. After practicing some challenging balancing as solitary trees, we offer some guidance to join "branches" (i.e. their upraised arms, lightly touching) and share some of each other's weight to become stronger and more solid in their places. Again, we are observant and respectful of the groups' comfort with touch and personal space, encouraging what amount of "support" feels safe. Processing questions explore the benefits of leaning on each other for strength and balance. Here is the complete prompt:

> Let's all circle up for this activity. Imagine that you are a tree, firmly rooted in the earth. Notice your trunk solid and strong. Notice your roots growing down in the ground, keeping you attached and steady. When you feel steady and ready, notice your branches that reach out to explore the atmosphere and what grows around you. Next, we're going to practice how to become an even more strong and balanced tree. You can either stretch your branches high or bring them to the side, or to your trunk. Pull one root from your right side [gently lift right foot a few inches]. Let's see if we can be still trees for 10 seconds. Good! Let's try the other side…Okay, let's try this! Keeping your left root above the ground, extend your branches out to the side to connect to another tree next to you. We are forming a grove of trees! What is your balance like now? What would happen if we added a small breeze to our grove? Just as in this activity, being in groups and being connected to others can help us feel stronger and more balanced, and it's also important to practice our personal strength and balance when we are by ourselves and being uniquely ourselves.

The Appreciations Circle

In this exercise, each student will become the focus of attention as they, ideally, receive a heartfelt appreciation from each member of the group, one at a time. Usually, we book-end the appreciations for each student by having one co-leader go first and the other go last. Preparing for the appreciation activity with the group is vital. Fierceness is essential to protect the vulnerability of each student in this challenge. We encourage the leaders to describe the seriousness of the activity, while helping the students to feel prepared, confident, and excited to participate. We take time to explore what appreciations are, noting the difference between complimenting someone on their external appearance versus their internal characteristics. For example, "If you like someone's clothing or style, what does that say about their courage to be unique or their creativity to dress colorfully?" Another example might be, "If you say someone is 'nice,' what things do you notice that show they are nice?" Here is the complete prompt:

> We've learned a lot about each other these past 8 weeks! And one thing we can give each other to help support each other is simply appreciations.

Appreciations give us a chance to share what we admire about each other, what we have learned from each other, and what we have enjoyed about each other. We hear enough criticisms all the time just walking down the hallway at school, what we want to do in this moment is something different: We want each of us to feel stronger by being noticed and appreciated in a good way.

There are different kinds and levels of appreciations: We can appreciate someone's shoes or we can say they are cool. But in this group, we want you to think of one thing you have noticed about each other, one thing you have learned, one thing that each person has done for you, or one thing you admire. I'll give an example by appreciating my co-leader. Jeff, you are so supportive of me and you give great feedback, both in what I do well and also in what I can improve on. Thank you for being such a great co-leader. Notice that I looked right at Jeff, used "I" language, and gave a good example of what I meant. Okay here we go: each person will receive and appreciation from everyone in the group. It can be a challenge to receive these, so please take a breath and try to let these good things in…

After each person receives their appreciations, we will do a little game to unwind: We'll do a shakedown starting from 7. We may pretend we are playing our favorite instrument in a rock band or have a dance party or strike a superhero pose.

Some groups choose to have quiet moments to think about each member and take notes so they are ready in the moment. Other methods to prepare the group include preparing a list of adjectives (e.g. bright, happy, helpful, smart, confident, brave, friendly, talented, generous, etc.) or sentence stems, as in the following list:

"I noticed in the group when you…"
"One thing I appreciate you is…"
"One thing I notice about you is…"
"I appreciated when you…"
"One thing you are really good at is…"

We recognize the risk and potentially damaging effects of a student receiving only cursory compliments or compliments that actually feel like put-downs (For example, "I guess you are nice?"). We do our best to make it clear, with our fierce leadership style, that such comments will not be tolerated and we set clear expectations for positive participation. If the group has particularly challenging students in it, we may set the norm that each student will receive three compliments (and as co-leaders we provide two of them), but that everyone must provide at least one during the whole exercise. Usually, more students eventually want to jump in with positive compliments and we allow and balance as best we can.

Understandably, even after several weeks in the group, not all students know each other well. Additionally, we don't expect that all students will be best friends after the group. It is still possible to help every student in the group receive positive appreciations, as in the following example:

Savon: Octavio, you inspire me because you are funny and nice.

Natalie: Octavio, I appreciate you in the group because you are funny and caring.

[It is now Arianna's turn to give a compliment to Octavio, but she remains silent]

Leader: Arianna, do you need more time to think? I can go.

Arianna: Yeah, I do.

Leader: Okay. Octavio I have noticed you are like…a quiet observer is what I think about. I think you're always present and you're always thinking about things and taking it in, and you're very composed, and I really appreciate your presence. Any time you share with the group I feel like it's very impactful.

Arianna: I don't really know what to say.

Leader: It's okay you can have some more time to think about it.

Arianna: I don't know. He's just quiet. I don't know.

Leader: Okay, you can say, "I appreciate you for being a good listener and for being respectful and not talking over others."

Arianna: I appreciate him for being respectful.

Leader: Please look at him and tell him directly…

Arianna: Um. I appreciate you, Octavio, for being respectful.

Leader: Alright, moving on to compliments for Abdullah. He looks really excited!

In this example, the leader uses a few strategies to help this challenging moment for Octavio become a positive one: She allows Arianna to pass; she models an example of a rich and positive appreciation; and she offers language to Arianna to give Octavio a genuine appreciation in a direct way.

In another strategic move, we create multiple breaks and moments of play to allow students to relax a bit and let down their guard in-between the more focused and serious moments when each student is receiving appreciations. Here are some examples of these playful breaks: (1) We ask them to pick an instrument of their choice and then play together, miming a silent rock band; (2) We ask them to pick their favorite superhero and then strike an appropriate pose or action; (3) We ask them to balance on one foot, if they can, and then jump up and down or flap their arms like a bird; (4) We may choose to move the group to a different location in the building between each student's appreciations, perhaps walking silently backward. The laughter and movement create intentional disruptions in the tension and focus they're asked to hold during the appreciations exercise.

These appreciations shared between the students often evoke deep emotions and real anxieties. Leaders are balancing both support and challenge to help the sixth graders remain with the experience, as in the example below:

Leader: Amaya, I have only spent a short time with you in this group and have not really seen you outside of this group, but I can tell that you also have a great fierceness. You are able to be the one in your friend group who takes charge and takes the lead. You have a power within you that I can hear, even if you don't voice it aloud. That is something that is very powerful and awesome.
[Amaya starts to cry and takes a big breath in]

Leader: If you would like, we could go for a walk. Or are you okay to stay?
[Amaya nods her head, signaling she is okay to stay in the group]

Leader: I think one of your biggest strengths is your emotions. I think that, I can guarantee you that you can connect with others and really empathize with them. I think that this can be a challenge at times, but it is a good thing and I really appreciate that about you. I so appreciate you sitting in that chair and participating in this.

In this example, our leaders are navigating the student's capacity to experience emotion in a group setting, offering validation and an invitation to take a break, yet ultimately reinforcing the courage to stay and be valued for being an empathetic and emotional person. One leader describes succinctly the support and challenge inherent in this activity. In the following transcript, our leaders show another example of how they help facilitate this process of both giving and receiving appreciations:

Leader: Who's going to be our brave first person to accept appreciations? You will, Wilson? Okay, take a minute now, and think about Wilson – what Wilson brings to school, to this group, and then whoever feels ready to start, we can hand over our phone for you to speak into so we can record it.

Luisa: I just like the fact that you...

Leader: Use Wilson's name and say it directly to him...

Luisa: I just like the way that you, Wilson, are not afraid to express your feelings and show emotion and the fact that you just like to stand up all the time. You're like, "I'll do it. I'll do this." So, yeah.

Devon: I was going to say the same exact one! You're always willing to jump in and be brave.

Leader: How is it for you to hear that, Wilson?

Wilson: I really liked it, because a lot of you said that I was really brave and um, sometimes I can feel that. Like even this spring break, we went hiking and I sat right next to a cliff with my dog. So I could really feel that bravery, even though I was also at the same time worried.

Leader: Bravery is often in the accompaniment of fear. Facing what we are afraid of...

Wilson: Yeah...

In this example, Wilson is able to hear appreciations, make links to his own life and "own' the bravery that others see in him. As described, receiving appreciations offers risks and rewards. The students' teachers often report the students reentering the classroom after this session with smiles, seemingly lighter and more positive. Overall, the appreciations exercise is a refreshing exception to the experience of "roasting" and comparative social media culture so influential in the student's daily lives:

Leader: How did it feel to receive a compliment?

Illana: It made me feel happy.

Leader: Can you tell me more about that? Why did that make you feel happy?

Illana: It made me feel like I had value and worth.

Leader: Yes! When you're appreciated, it lets you know that you're seen and valued in your class, family, or friend group...it's the opposite of bullying. Instead of taking one aspect of someone and tearing them down, being appreciated allows someone to see that they have qualities that are important and valuable.

One leader highlighted how this positive experience of receiving appreciations was reflected in the responses two students gave in this session's weekly surveys:

> We have been able to make progress towards our group goal of increasing social connections and supportive relationships in our community. This was seen in our weekly survey results. We have two very honest but consistently lower raters (usually 2's and 3's, and only some 4's). After today's appreciations activity, they both felt very connected and respected in the group, giving mostly 5's.

We want to underline again how positive and yet challenging this activity can be. In one of our groups, for example, our leaders knew the appreciation activity would be very challenging for the students in their group. In particular, they knew it would be challenging for their students to make both positive and direct statements to each other without sarcasm or misdirection. To address this challenge, the leaders decided on an "indirect" approach, asking the students: "Which Pokemon would you pick to represent each member of this group and why?" As demonstrated in the transcript below, this allowed for the students to be surprisingly open and warm with each other:

Leader:	"Ok, everyone, now it's Sammy's turn to receive appreciations. Alex, would you go first?"
Alex:	"Sure. Hmmm, what's the nicest Pokemon? It's kind of hard to choose, I would pick just the nicest one there is because I think you are the nicest person ever for being there for me and helping me talk about my mental health."
Sammy:	"Well, thanks, Alex. I'm really glad you felt comfortable doing that."
Alex:	"Yeah it was just really awesome. I'm still working on it, but that just helped a lot."
Leader:	"That's so awesome, Alex. Thank you for sharing that, Sammy."

Reaping the rewards within this session is possible! Recognizing the risks students face and preparing them for this final challenge of connection is crucial to its success. Within this eighth session, students are able to be seen and acknowledged for their individual strengths and contributions while reciprocating with appreciations for their fellow group members. Our leaders carefully collect these appreciations and write them down on decorated cards that will be given out to each student in the groups during our last, closing session, described next.

Session 9

Closing the Group

Brief Instructions

Overview

The goal of our ninth session is to intentionally close the group in a positive light and give the students some reminders of what has been helpful for them from this group. In the "Opening," we revisit one of the various and perhaps favorite mindful activities from past sessions. In the "Body," we first review the sessions of past weeks before leading a closing activity using the image cards that have been used previously. In the "Closing," we provide each student with an "appreciation card" listing all the appreciations they received in Session 8. In addition to asking the students to complete the weekly survey, we also close by asking them to complete the "post-assessment."

Materials

- Animal Cards, Appreciation cards, Post-Assessments, Weekly Surveys

Opening

- Revisit a variation of favorite group activity (e.g. mindfulness activity, Alligator Swamp, etc.)

Body

- Tell a descriptive story about this group and what was covered each week, highlighting memorable moments
- Help participants share memories about what they remember and what was accomplished and learned
- Lead *Closing Cards* activity:
  "Pick three cards: one to represent something about your experience before we had this group, one to represent something about your experience in

DOI: 10.4324/9781003368779-13

this group, and one thing you can take with from this group back into your classroom/school/life…"

Closing

- Hand out *Appreciation Cards* and have group members:
- Each read them over quietly
- Each share one or more appreciations aloud
- Sign each other's card in "yearbook" style
- Complete weekly surveys
- Hand out, read through, and ask participants to complete "post-assessment"
- Remind participants this is the last meeting and review how group members can connect with each other outside of this group.

Reminders

- Acknowledge and accept various responses to group closing. Endings can be sad, and students have different ways of expression.
- Reflect intentionally on activities and growth made as a group and individuals, highlighting the skills gained. Skills learned in groups are transferable to other experiences.
- Be creative in making the Appreciation Cards. Explore individual responses to the kindness they received. The cards are tangible souvenirs of appreciations that can boost mood long after group ends.

Full Description

Endings can be hard, especially when what is ending has been a good thing. Many of the sixth graders we have worked with over the past nine weeks are not happy to see the group end. We don't claim that the groups are completely successful for every child with whom we have worked. We have found over time, however, that the groups as a whole are generally successful in making gains toward the two primary goals that we set out to accomplish from the beginning: to help them both belong and be themselves. That is, many of the sixth graders find the groups to be a supportive enough place to stick their necks out a bit more than they usually do in sixth-grade context. In so doing, they get a sense of having found their voice and use it to make statements and to make their opinions known in the group. They have also said things about themselves, about their likes and dislikes, about how they are both similar and different from others in the group, about how they have faced or seen bullying, and they have given appreciations to other members in the group (and received them as well) in a way that may have been a singularly positive and bolstering experience in their young lives.

By sticking their necks out and participating in our structured group activities, they have not only become more visible as individuals to the other group members (and to themselves), but they have also experienced real contact and connection with a group of related others. In short, many of them have, to some extent, felt a sense of belonging with others, a sense of knowing others, and of being known by others. These twin goals of differentiation (of the self) and integration (into the group) serve as two powerfully protective factors as they navigate the tricky terrain of middle school life. It is our hope that they can carry these centrally important experiences with them as they leave the group: That they now know a bit more about how to be themselves and stand on their own two feet, while at the same time feeling known by and connected to others in healthy and supportive ways.

After we spend some time reviewing where we have been and what we have done as a group over the past eight weeks, we start the closing card activity that is the centerpiece of our last group session. We begin by asking the students to pick three images from the myriad of laminated picture cards spread out before them: one to represent something about their experience before the group started, one to represent something about their experience in the group, and one to represent something they want to take with them from the group. A theme that tends to emerge from this activity is related to the experience we described above, the experience of moving from a lack of connection to one of feeling stronger in themselves and in their relationships with others. The decks of laminated cards we use are collections of all kinds of images, animals, people, places, weather systems, etc.

One boy, Chris, picked three animal images (which we show in modified sketches in Figure 8) and then used them to describe his experience, before, during, and after the group.

Showing his three cards one at a time, Chris shares:

> Before the group, I was in my egg. I was just with my group of friends. And I didn't really get out of my egg. But then during the group, I did. I was just a small animal, and I kind of ventured out from my friend group. And I got a couple of friends, but not huge friends. But now I learned how to stand up to bullies and I'm trying to find new friends as well.

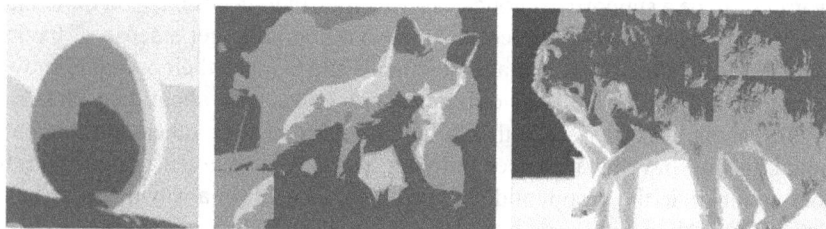

Figure 8 Qualitative Data Example 3 – Closing Card Activity

It is interesting to note that Chris's third image, in which two wary wolves circle one another, can be seen as holding the theme of both cooperation and fierceness that we have used throughout this text to highlight the dual nature of social skills that are necessary to develop. Describing a related theme regarding how it takes courage to be assertive in making new friends, Jen shared the following in a different group:

> In the beginning of the group, I always talked to the same people [She shows a picture of three lions snuggled close together]. I was really close to those people and I didn't really want to meet new people because I was too scared to. Then [she shows a picture of an awkward looking bird], I was like confused if I should meet new people because what if they don't like the same things I liked. It would be hard talking to them. So, I was just thinking. And then by the end of the group, what I will take with me is that it's okay to be different. And even if I am different [she shows a humorous picture of a polar bear] it is still fun to talk to new people.

One boy, Daniel, shared that, "Before group, I felt caged in" and shared that during group he felt "togetherness." Another girl, Esther, said, "In the beginning of group, I felt empty" (showing a picture of a wide open field), and then showed a picture of a group of kids together, stating, "This is when we're all friends." Another boy, Bruce, shared, "I felt like a statue because I didn't really want to stand out or participate in group. And now I am an owl because I know more and I pay attention because I really like group." Natalia showed her three cards and said, "Before group I was calm like the lake and flower, with no movement. I'm opposite now. I am like the tiger, it's strong and fierce, yet I am also the butterfly which is calm." And one of the sweetest sets of images came from Willa, who first showed a card of skiers coming down a steep mountain and said, "First, I felt challenged. Then, I felt more wanted [showing a picture of a baby strapped to her mother's back]. This is when we got along with each other [picture of a group campfire]."

We have learned over time that this card exercise elicits metaphors of rich emotive quality that would be hard to come by without the aid of the images they get to choose from. This very personal and qualitative data is helpful for our leaders to get a sense of the impact these groups have had on the children. The examples such as those we shared above are also effective to present to the teachers, principals, and other administration officials with whom we want to share the effect our groups are having on their students.

In addition to the qualitative data, however, we also make sure to collect and share quantitative data that represents a broader view of all the children's experiences in these groups. As we described in the opening sections of this book, we do this in three ways: We collect *pre- and post-assessment* data from the first session and the last session of the groups as well as weekly survey data from each week of the group. We generally find a significant and positive effect for most groups between their pre-test and their post-test assessments as well as generally more positive responses to the weekly surveys over the nine weeks. Table 8 shows the weekly survey results of nine groups that we ran concurrently for one term. Note that while some groups average lower scores than others, the majority do follow a pattern.

Generally speaking, students tend to respond more favorably to the weekly survey questions in the first few weeks and the last few weeks of group with a tendency being for the middle sessions receiving slightly lower scores. We make sense of this "bowl shaped" tendency in that those middle sessions are intentionally more challenging given we are addressing difficult to talk about subjects such as what children tend to get bullied for and what strategies have worked and not worked in the face of such discrimination. Understandably, these topics are more difficult to address and certainly less fun than Week Two's *Alligator Swamp* team-building activity and lacking the sweetness of Week Eight's *Appreciations Circle* activity.

On average, then, the overall data from our diverse groups tends to look something like the line, representing data from one recent group, in Table 9. We take this as a good sign: we are both challenging our sixth graders appropriately and we are supporting them to have a shared experience in which they feel seen and connected by the time the groups have run their course.

We are consistently using both the qualitative and quantitative data we collect to both report out to stakeholders and also to revise and strengthen the curriculum of our groups. We have made numerous changes to our weekly sessions over time and will continue to do as we move forward. Some pieces of the curriculum have remained stable and consistently received well over time, such as the way

Table 8 Quantitative Data Example 1 – Weekly Survey Averages, Nine Groups

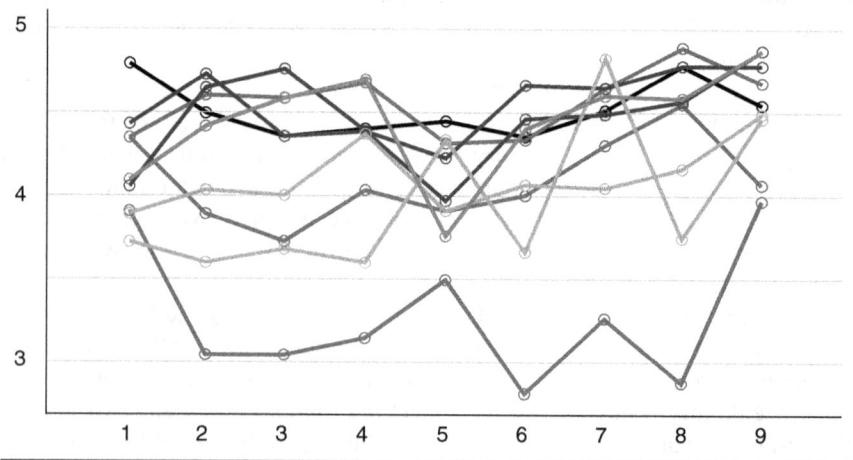

Table 9 Quantitative Data Example 2 – Weekly Survey Averages, One Group

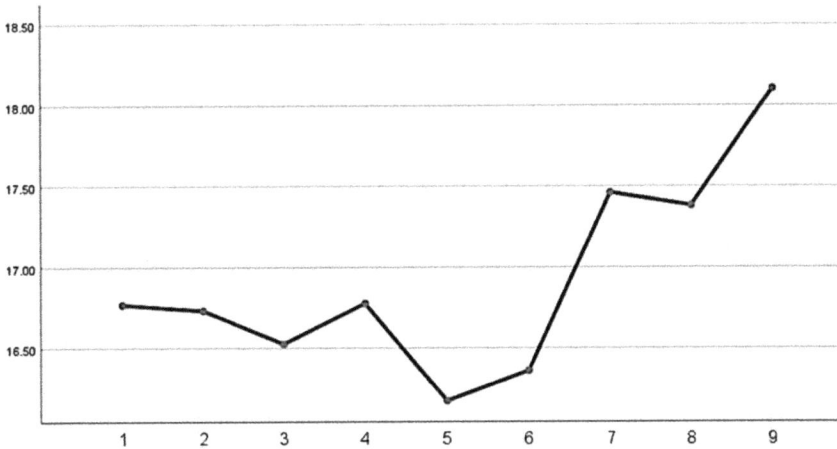

we open groups (with the *60-Second Autobiography*), the fun and challenging *Alligator Swamp* activity, as well as the way we end the groups with the *Appreciations Circle* in Week 8 and the *Card Activity* in Week 9.

A second kind of card activity that we use as the last piece of the last session of our groups involves individual cards that our leaders have made for each individual in their groups. On these cards, our leaders have written down each appreciation that the child received in Week 8, as well as added appreciations from the group leaders. These appreciation cards are distributed as the group is ready to close and the leaders ask each child to silently read each appreciation they find on their card. After a few silent moments in which we see shy smiles on many faces, the leaders ask the children to choose one appreciation from their card to share with the rest of the group, such as one they have never heard about themselves before or one they just like a lot. Our last session ends with each child saying one affirming thing about themselves that someone else in the group has seen and recognized. In this way, to the very end, we are working to reinforce our two primary goals for the group overall: that each child can become stronger in themselves as individuals, and at the same time, more connected to others as members of a supportive group.

Part Three

Strategic Story Examples

Overview

In Part Three of this text, we provide an additional resource which is meant to be used in tandem with the curriculum. We provide a collection of 40 strategic stories on four different themes which have been contributed by Lewis & Clark Graduate School faculty and students and have been used as a significant part of the curriculum (described in Part Two). These strategic stories can be used "as is" in any *Belong and Be You* counseling group, but are also provided as inspirational examples of how a group leader can construct their own strategic stories for use in groups.

DOI: 10.4324/9781003368779-14

Managing Emotions
Strategic Story Examples

Overview

Managing our strong emotions is not an easy task. Not only are there many different types of feelings to be sorted out (anger, anxiety, grief, sadness, etc.), but also we have to figure out what to do with them once we identify them. How do you express anger or anxiety without making the situation worse? How can we come up with words when we need them instead of either shutting down or acting out? These are the kinds of complex issues we help our sixth-graders work through with the help of the following kinds of strategic stories on this topic.

Broken Toes

When I was in eighth grade, I had a backpack that I would bring to school every day and I also had a sports bag that I would sometimes carry to school on days when I had a baseball game. I remember one Sunday night I was packing up my backpack and getting ready for school the next day. The sports bag was on the floor next to me, but I didn't need it for the next day, so it sat empty. My brother, who was two years younger than me in school and also played sports, came into my room and asked me if he could borrow the sports bag. I guess I was not feeling very generous, because I said no. He left the room, but he came back in a few minutes and said, "You're not even using the bag tomorrow and I need it, so can I please use it?!" Once again, I said no. I picked up the sports bag and started pretending I was packing it up for school the next day. My brother stormed out of the room and I put the sports bag back down on the floor. About a minute later, my brother came running into my room, grabbed the sports bag, and started to run out of the room with the bag in his hand.

You know in those cartoons when they show somebody get so mad that steam comes out of the ears and flames come off the top of their heads? Well, that was me in that moment. I was so mad that I chased him to the door of my room and just as he was stepping through the doorway, I shoved him from behind. He lost his balance, went flying across the hall, and smashed his foot into the opposite

DOI: 10.4324/9781003368779-15

wall, making an ugly crunching sound as he did. When I looked down at his foot a moment later, to my horror I saw blood oozing up between his toes and I knew something bad had happened, and I had done it.

In that moment, I just wished I could take back the last 30 seconds of my life and have a "do over." But I couldn't. I had broken my brother's toes and I felt horrible! I had been so angry, but now I was so sickened and feeling so much guilt and shame. I felt so sorry for hurting my brother. By pushing him in anger, I had caused him significant harm, all because of a stupid sports bag!

Thankfully, my brother eventually healed, maybe even forgave me, and we are still good friends today. But I am telling you this story because I wish I had been better able to deal with my emotions in a way that wouldn't have caused so much injury to my brother and so much shame to me! I wish I had known then what I know now about how to identify my feelings at the time I am feeling them, how to help myself cool down when I am feeling a particularly strong feeling, and what actions I can take when I am having strong emotions in order to resolve the situation I find myself in with a more peaceful solution. We will talk more about these strategies during group today.

The Crooked Paintings

I want to tell you a story about when I was in sixth grade. I became best friends with my neighbor Brittany that year. We went to the same school all through elementary school, but we were never in the same class. Starting in sixth grade, we walked to school together every morning. After school, I would stay at her house until my parents came home so I didn't have to go to daycare anymore. We did *everything* together. Going to the movies, having sleepovers, talking about cute boys. Everything.

When I was in middle school, I really hated to do homework. I didn't think it was fair that I spent all day at school and then still had to do more work in the evenings and on weekends. I would put off all my homework until the very last minute, then hurry to get it done before bed. My parents didn't like that much, so they made up rules, like I had to finish my homework for the weekend before going to do things with my friends.

One Saturday afternoon, I got a call from Brittany asking if I could go to the movies with her that night. A new superhero movie had just come out and we were both excited to see it. I told her I'd ask my parents if I could go and give her a call right back. I ran up the stairs to my parent's room and asked if I could go to the movies with Brittany that night.

Of course my mom immediately asked, "Did you do all your homework?" This was always her first question when I wanted to do something fun with my friends. "Not yet! But I can finish it on Sunday," I said. I knew I didn't have that much homework to do and I thought I could definitely finish it in one day. "You know the rules. If you finish your homework today, you can do whatever you want with the rest of your weekend," said my mom. She was always so strict with the rules! "But Brittany's going to the movies tonight! She's going to do her homework tomorrow, not tonight. Can't I just go this once? I promise I'll finish my homework tomorrow!" I pleaded.

My mom stayed firm. "Absolutely not. You know the rules. If you start your homework now, maybe you can finish before Brittany leaves for the movies." I felt my face getting hot. My mother was always so unreasonable! I had a perfectly good plan for getting my homework done, but my mom just wouldn't bend the rules! "This is so stupid!" I yelled. "You never let me do anything fun!" I stormed out of the room and ran downstairs. My whole body felt like it was vibrating and I felt like my hands were full of electricity. Tears welled up in my eyes and I knew I was going to start crying soon.

I stomped into the kitchen and grabbed a cup to fill with water, hoping it would calm me down. It didn't work. I was shaking and felt like I wanted to break something. Holding the cup in my hand, I thought about smashing it on the floor, sending pieces of glass skittering across the tile. In the back of my mind, I knew if I threw the glass and broke it, I'd have to clean it all up. I might even step on some pieces and hurt myself. And I definitely would get in trouble and wouldn't be able to go to the movies.

The tears I'd been holding back started to fall, dripping down my face. It just felt so unfair! I wanted my mom to know how mad and upset I was at her, but I knew smashing the cup was a bad idea. Looking wildly around the kitchen, I suddenly had an idea! My mom is an artist and hung art on the walls all around the house. She was very particular about keeping all the pictures exactly straight. When my dad would bump into one, she'd notice right away and line it up again so it was perfectly straight. She always wanted the house to look organized and perfect in case guests dropped by.

That was it! I knew in a flash how I was going to get back at her for not letting me go to the movies! I rushed through the kitchen and living room, tilting each picture just a little bit, until everything was slightly off kilter. It felt like a huge relief, doing something to upset my mom when she'd been so unfair. In the living room, I stepped back to admire my handiwork and felt satisfied with what I'd done. I let out a big sigh, went looking for some tissues to dry my tears and blow my nose. Then I pulled out my homework and got to work. I was going to make it to that movie no matter what.

I wanted to tell you this story today because I know how difficult it can be to navigate through big feelings when we have them. I'd love to know what you think about how I handled my emotions in this situation.

"You Go First"

I'm going to tell a story about when I was around your age, are you all ready to listen to my story? Great, because this is pretty hard for me, so I appreciate your being willing to listen. I know this group is really good at giving each other space to share without making fun of anyone, so I trust you.

When I was a teenager, there was a summer camp that kids in my area would go to every summer. We would drive out about an hour into the woods, to Little River Camp. There was a swimming hole, which is a nice deep slow spot in the river where we could swim. There was a big field for games, and they had cabins with bunk beds for sleeping. I had been to the camp a few times in middle school as a camper, but this year I was there as one of the counselors. I was not very old, probably about 14 or 15, and the kids were I think fourth or fifth graders, so not much age difference between us. I was nervous because even though I was supposed to be helping to be in charge of the kids, I didn't feel grown up or like I knew what I was doing at all. As part of our camp counselor job, we were going to run a small group, kind of like what we're doing here, except that no one really helped us figure out what we were supposed to do or talk about. My co-leader's name was Allison, and she was really nice, and my same age, but somehow seemed so much more grown up and confident than I felt.

Our first day of small group, we took our campers to the far side of the field to sit together in the gazebo and try to get to know each other. Allison suggested a game where we go around and each say our name, and an adjective starting with the same letter as our name, that describes us. I was already nervous to begin with, but when she said that I felt a little panicky, because I didn't know what an adjective was. A million thoughts went through my mind in a few seconds; thinking about how I was home schooled and my parents hadn't thought it was important to teach me about adjectives and nouns and verbs and things like that, thinking about how stupid I felt not knowing something I was sure everyone else there knew, even the kids that were younger than me, and frantically trying to make a plan so nobody would find out that I didn't know something I was supposed to know. I did what I have done many times in that type of situation, I decided to just keep quiet, listen to what others were saying, and try to figure out what I was supposed to do by listening to them. All of those thoughts and feelings must have run through my head in the few seconds after Allison described the game, because after she was done talking she turned to me and said, "Amanda, why don't you go first!" I froze. I had no idea what to do, and I couldn't think of any words to say. I had no plan, and just saying "I don't know what an adjective is" didn't occur to me as an option, because it felt like I might die if people found out I didn't know something they all did. I must have looked terrified and I know my face and chest turned red, because that still happens now when I have strong feelings or get embarrassed. Allison must have seen how scared I was and realized that I didn't know what to do, because she said, "You know, an adjective, a describing word. Like Amazing Amanda." I was so grateful to her for helping me out, but that shame and fear stayed in my body for a long time after that. I still feel it now when I think about this story.

In that moment, I felt stuck, like I didn't have any choice but to hide or the shame would get bigger and overwhelm me. I wonder now if there were other options that I couldn't think of because I was so afraid and frozen. One big thing I see in this story that I couldn't see at the time is the value and support that is available from friends. Allison was right there, ready to help me, even though I couldn't ask. I feel like only recently, with my classmates in grad school, have I been able to really practice trusting my friends and asking for help or saying "I don't know what that means." And every time I say that to my classmates, they take the opportunity to step up and help me, and usually someone else says "I'm glad you asked that, because I didn't know either."

I am telling you this story today because figuring out how to manage strong emotions can be overwhelming. We all can have strong feelings: anger, sadness, in my case, shame and fear. And I want you to know it's normal and part of being a human person to struggle to figure out what to do with those emotions when they come up. It's also normal to feel stuck, like we have to figure it all out ourselves without telling anyone. But if we can find someone we trust to share the big feelings with, it can make the feelings less overwhelming, and it can give someone a chance to show us love and support.

"Emotions Are a Natural Thing."

When I was in third grade, my brother, who was 23 years old at the time, got into a car accident and passed away. The very next day after he died, my class was planning a field trip to this place in the mountains called Windwolves Preserve in California where we were going to go hiking, learn how to track animals, and spend all day in nature. For weeks I have been so excited to go on this field trip because I loved hiking and spending time outside. To me, at that time it was way better than being inside a classroom all day. When the day came, I was overwhelmed with sadness about the loss of my brother but I knew I still wanted to go. I convinced my parents to let me go and they allowed me after we explained the situation to my teacher. We loaded onto the bus and off we went. Once we arrived, we hiked under this huge tree to eat our lunch. During lunch, my teacher came up to me and asked how I was doing and I remember I just felt this lump in my throat because I had to think back to everything that happened the day before. I immediately started crying and then got so embarrassed that all my classmates were watching me cry. Well, fast forward to the following day back at school: I was still so embarrassed that everyone had watched me cry. That embarrassment stayed with me for about a week until I ended up forgetting about it. I am telling you all this story because emotions are a natural thing for all of us and it is important to express them in a healthy way. It may feel embarrassing or shameful at the time but that passes even if it feels like it won't.

New at School

I'm going to tell you all a story about when I was in middle school – it was when I was in eighth grade, so a little bit older than you all are now, but it still feels hard for me to talk about, even now. Do we all think we're ready to listen to the story? Thanks in advance for being respectful!

The summer before eighth grade, my family and I moved from Portland to a smaller town on the coast called Wheeler. I was sad to leave my Portland friends, but kind of excited to meet new people and start "fresh" in a new town. I never felt quite comfortable in sixth and seventh grades, like I didn't quite have the right clothes or personality or was cool enough, so I kind of thought that by being somewhere new, I could be new also.

I remember my first day of eighth grade being so excited and nervous to see the new building and meet all my new classmates. I picked out a new outfit to wear and made sure my make-up looked good. My mom dropped me off and right away I could feel everyone looking at me. My school wasn't that big, so having a new student was something everyone noticed pretty quickly. Since it was the first day, there was a big orientation assembly for everyone. I remember feeling really nervous about who I was going to sit next to or if anyone was going to talk to me. Thankfully, it was during my math class, so I had to sit next to my classmates from that class and the teacher decided who we sat next to. The assembly made me realize that I really needed to be worried about who I was going to sit next to during lunch since there wasn't going to be a teacher assigning seats.

When lunch finally rolled around, I remember walking in with my bagged lunch and my favorite drink at the time – Diet Coke. Before I even found a table, I realized that everyone else was drinking Sierra Mist, Pepsi, and Mountain Dew – no diet soda anywhere! As I walked between the tables, no one seemed to want to let me sit with them and I noticed some people whispering as I went by. I felt like a total outsider. I finally found a spot by myself at the end of a table, and I got my lunch out. I felt so embarrassed that I was alone and I could tell I was blushing. I drank my Diet Coke and suddenly felt stupid for having such an "adult" drink.

I probably lasted three minutes at the table until I couldn't take it anymore. I grabbed my lunch and went to the safest place I could think of – the bathroom. I ended up spending the rest of that lunch eating alone in a bathroom stall holding back tears. Nothing was going as I planned! I wasn't a new person – I was still as lame and awkward as I had been in Portland!

When I saw my mom after school, I tried to pretend everything was okay and that I made a lot of friends, but I couldn't fake it and ended up crying to her for a while. She held me on the couch and told me that it would just take time and I would make friends one day. It took a month or two, but I eventually found a group of friends that I liked and who were nice to me. People began to see me as Bella instead of the "new girl." Now, I am still best friends with some of the people that I met in Astoria. One thing I learned after that experience of being the "new kid," was that I always made sure to at least say "hi" to any new person at school.

I'm telling you all this for two reasons: First, to remember that hard moments, hard days, or even hard weeks will always pass. I wish I could say everything was great at the beginning of eighth grade, but honestly, it took a little bit for me to find my place. But I did find it. Secondly, I want to remind you all of the power that a smile or a kind word can have for someone who seems like they're struggling. I remember so vividly the relief I felt in those early days when someone was nice to me. It doesn't take much effort and it can really turn someone's day around."

Special Shoes

This is a story from when I was in middle school that I want to share with the group today. I went to Spencer Middle School. When I was in seventh grade, my whole world was soccer. I played soccer as much as I could and most of my best friends played with me too. When I heard that I could play indoor soccer during the winter I was so excited! Normally I would play other sports in the winter but now I could play soccer year-round. When playing indoor soccer you need different shoes. You can't wear the normal cleats like when you play outside – remember this!

After finding out that I was signed up to play, I told my best friend Ryan that he should join the team. He was extremely excited, and his parents signed him up immediately. Later that week, while waiting for my mom to pick us up from school we started to talk about how much we were looking forward to playing together. Talking about all the goals we were going to score and also the excitement of trying this new variation of soccer.

An important detail about Ryan is that he grew up in a house where money was very tight. Sometimes Ryan got really stressed out if he needed to buy school supplies, new sporting equipment, or other things. So, when I told him that to play indoor soccer you needed new, special shoes and couldn't use your normal cleats, it made him anxious and sad. Ryan got worried that he wasn't going to be able to play because his parents couldn't afford to buy him new shoes. I could see that Ryan was starting to get worried. He was pacing around and the smile on his face changed to a worried look. Instead of comforting Ryan, I decided to repeat that he really needed these special shoes, or he wouldn't be on the team. Thinking back, I don't know why I said that to him, but I did. And Ryan began to cry. He was so sad thinking he wasn't going to play soccer with his friends. As Ryan cried, I chose not to do anything. I don't know why I didn't do anything. Maybe Ryan beat me at something earlier that day or said something that was kind of hurtful. Either way it didn't feel good to see my best friend so sad and distraught. But I also didn't do anything to help him.

Soon after, my mom arrived and gave Ryan a big hug. I explained why he was crying, and my mom helped soothe him by saying it was going to be okay and that there were many options for him. He could even wear his current shoes, if need be, and it wouldn't matter. Thinking back, this story really stands out in my mind. I can remember exactly where we were standing (on the front lawn by the oak tree) and Ryan's face when he realized that he might not be able to play. I wanted to tell you this story because I don't believe I did the right thing. Ryan was my best friend and I watched him get sadder and sadder and I chose not to act in a way to comfort him. Sometimes our best friends – or other people we care about – have really difficult feelings (just like us) and there are clues that are telling us how they are feeling. I feel that I didn't respond to his intense emotions in a way that was kind or helpful. Honestly, I made it worse for Ryan.

"Mostly, I Was Jealous."

I am the youngest of three children. My brother is four years older than me, and my sister is six years older than me. Because of our age difference, when I was growing up, we never really got along. I think they thought I was too young and annoying to want to hang out with me or get to know me. I remember wanting to be friends with my sister. By the time I was in middle school, my sister had kind of stopped talking to me. My sister did not like me coming into her room, and she did not want me to be around her at family gatherings. I do not even remember her talking to me at dinner. My brother was always busy with sports or his friends, so he was never around. I was lonely.

One day, when I was in the sixth grade, I invited my friend over to my house. My friend had been sick for a long time. When we were in third grade, she had been diagnosed with Leukemia. She was always in and out of the hospital and having to miss school. Sometimes her immune system was weak from chemo, so she could not be near the other students. I remember on this particular day that she felt better than she had in a while, and I thought it would be fun to hang out with her.

After school, my friend and I went to my house, and we hung out and were just having fun. Soon, my sister came home from school. With my sister home, it felt like my friend just wanted to be with her. She asked her if we could come into her room. My sister let us. I remember sitting in my sister's room, thinking it was weird to sit there because I never was allowed in. My friend sat next to my sister during dinner, and they spent most of the dinner talking. I remember feeling confused because I was mad at my sister for treating my friend better than she treated me. I was angry at my friend for wanting to hang out with my sister. However, mostly I was jealous. I was upset I almost ended my friendship right then and there.

I remember having a conversation with my mom about what I was feeling later, and she reminded me of the struggles my friend was facing. She also said that my sister was trying to make my friend feel welcomed and supported. My mom also reminded me that my friend did not have an older sister, so it was probably nice to have an older girl to talk to. After talking to my mom, I still felt mad and jealous, but I also felt a little better. It was almost like the emotions did not have such a hold on me as they did before our conversation. I knew that soon I would not be so mad or jealous. There was also the bonus of not losing a friend.

I am telling you this story because sometimes we will become mad or jealous, and we might want to do something big, to take some kind of action to help ourselves feel better. It might be hard even to see straight in these moments, and that can be tough and maybe a bit scary. I want you to know that it is okay to have overwhelming emotions. Moreover, you do not have to go through it alone. Do not be afraid to find comfort and understanding by talking with a friend, a family member, or a teacher.

"I Actually Punched Her in the Eye!"

When I was in seventh grade, I had this frenemy named Stephanie. Sometimes we would get along and other times she got on my nerves. One day, we were in PE and she kept teasing me by saying that my arms had too much hair on them. Our friends took it as a joke, but it actually hurt my feelings and made me feel really angry and annoyed. Then, she took it a step further and grabbed the hair on my arm, laughing as she plucked it out. This turned into a regular thing and every day in PE she would do the same thing, teasing me more and more and even nicknaming me "wolverine." I pretended it didn't bother me for about a week. Then one day, she shouted "wolverine!" in front of this group of cooler kids and everyone started calling me that in class.

I decided to give my friend the cold shoulder and ignore her. She tapped my shoulder in the locker room and tried to ask me about our next class. I told her to ask someone else. She kept pestering me and pestering me, maybe not realizing that I was angry with her. I couldn't take it anymore and I screamed at her to leave me alone and I actually punched her in the eye! I felt like I had lost control and immediately regretted it. She started crying and told our teacher what happened and I was sent to the office. Afterward I felt so bad, I didn't mean to hurt her, but I felt so angry inside and didn't know what to do at the moment. Looking back, I wish that I had talked to her about how her comments made me feel. I also wish I had stood up for myself instead of bottling how I felt and then exploding which resulted in consequences for both her and me. I had let anger get the best of me.

The reason I'm telling this story is because sometimes we have intense, strong emotions and if we act on them, we feel out of control. For me, it has been really important to learn to recognize those emotions and then manage them in a healthy way so that I don't hurt people or get hurt myself resulting in serious consequences. I hope we can talk about how we learn to know when we are having strong feelings and what we can do to express them in healthy ways.

"I Can Hear My Voice Shaking."

When I was in middle school, I experienced a lot of anxiety, but I thought I had a way around it. If I pushed the worry away, then it would somehow disappear. For a long time, it did seem to magically disappear. I can remember that one day, I decided to try out for a play. To this day, I don't know why I auditioned! I guess that even though I have a part of me that is introverted and shy and anxious, there is another part of me that wants to stand up, perform, and be seen. In some ways, this story is about the struggle between those two parts of myself.

On the day of auditions, I walked into the auditorium and I sat in a scratchy chair with gum stuck underneath. I can remember my hand touching the gum and how gross that felt. I was super uncomfortable all of a sudden. Then it was almost my turn to audition. As I was waited in the wings for my turn, I felt like my body was on fire. I felt my heart pounding. I could feel myself sweating. I felt like lightning was running through my body. I was telling myself, "Don't mess up, don't mess up." But the more I pushed down my anxious feelings, the worse they got. I was frustrated and shaking, thinking, "Today of all days!"

One of my teachers must have seen how anxious I was. She pulled me aside and said, "I know you can do this, just do what you practiced." Those words made me feel both happy and frustrated. If I could just put those darn feelings aside and do what I know I could do! Someone had told me to take deep breaths, but that didn't seem to be working. Now, on top of everything else, I was feeling angry with myself for getting so anxious!

Then it was my audition time. I walk onto the stage and I notice the lights feel hot. I have never produced this much sweat in my entire life. I can hear my voice shaking as I'm reading my lines and singing. I feel everyone's eyes on me and I'm starting to get tired from all of the stress. I just want to go home.

A moment later, just like that, the audition is over. I feel the cold air on my face as I rush outside and I start to feel calm for the first time in a long time. A part of me is feeling proud: I had pushed through and had somehow survived it! Being on the other side of all that stress felt nice. But another part of me is still angry: Why did I have to ruin everything by getting so anxious?

I am telling you this story because I've learned that such strong feelings do not just "go away" all at once. It takes time to work through difficult emotions. Even when you feel like you are doing everything right to manage a strong feeling, sometimes it takes a while for the emotion to work its way through you. It also takes a lot of different tools to manage difficult emotions, and sometimes we will be able to use our tools and sometimes not. The most important thing is to be patient and supportive of ourselves, to keep doing the things we want to do to move us ahead (like my audition) while at the same time to try and keep learning how to manage challenging feelings we have. I hope we can learn more about how each of us manages our strong feelings, what works and what hasn't been so helpful.

"I Started to Be Very Unkind to Myself."

Growing up with divorced parents, I spent most of my childhood spending the weekdays with my mother and weekends at my father's house. My older sister, Jasmine, was living with my mother and me, while my older sister, Jade was living with my dad. When I was entering the fifth grade, I began living with my father permanently and my mother moved to California with my sister, Jasmine. As much as I wanted to stay with my mom, she was unable to take care of me and my parents agreed that I would be better living with my dad.

Another thing that was happening in my life was that every school year, I transferred to a different school. Sixth grade was the first year that I did not move. Sixth grade was a very big year for me in terms of learning to make friends, getting used to the idea of not moving, and missing my mom. It had been two years since I had seen my mom after living with her for nearly seven years. I had to adjust to my father's parenting, and now the fact that he remarried and I all of a sudden had step sisters. My whole family dynamic had changed, and I was feeling really big emotions that I did not know how to grasp. I felt abandoned by my mother. There were many nights where I wondered why she couldn't take me with her while my other sister was able to. I also felt anger towards my father for replacing my mother with my stepmother. I already had a mother and two older sisters, and I did not need another family.

During this time, I struggled to talk to my parents and even my sisters about what I was feeling. My sisters were much older than me, and had their own lives to focus on. I did not speak to my mother much at this time because I was holding so many negative emotions and I could not bring myself to forgive her for leaving me and with my father. He was working very long days and by the time he came home, he would not have much energy to talk to me. I felt very lonely while I was trying to navigate through all of my emotions, on top of trying to be a good student and trying to maintain my friendships. With me moving around so much in the past, I struggled to understand what having friends meant, considering I never stuck around long enough to develop genuine connections with others.

My body was being pulled in multiple directions that prevented me from feeling happy. I began turning inward because I felt like I had no control over anything that was happening in my life. I also felt like I had no one to talk to. Somehow, I began to feel that I must be the problem. I felt like there was something wrong with me that prevented me from being happy like I thought my classmates were. I started to be very unkind to myself and I began to hurt my own body. I was unsure of how else to cope with the things I was feeling, and I took it out on myself. This went on for a few months before my sister saw the scratches on my arm and told my father. My family was heartbroken when they saw that I was hurting myself. They could not understand why I couldn't come to them with my problems.

I wanted to share this story because I remember being in the sixth grade and feeling like no one was going to be able to understand all the emotions that I was feeling. I also know that the world can feel like it is ending when you are experiencing multiple things at the same time, like I was. I want you to know that I know that feelings are not easy to navigate through alone. Even though you may not feel it at the time, there is always someone who you can reach out to talk to. Someone who will listen to you and help make you feel better. I hope we can talk about the people in your life you can reach out to, and maybe some of those you haven't even thought of yet.

Addressing Bullying
Strategic Story Examples

Overview

We use the following kinds of stories to address the many issues and complexities related to bullying. We offer stories about how we were once in the role of the bully and why. We ask them to consider situations where they are witnessing one person bully another and what, if anything, they can do about it. We try to help them make sense of difficult issues like the difference between bullying and teasing. We also try to be honest about the all-too-common bind they may find themselves in that bullying can get worse if they do nothing or actually ask for help. Overall, we work to help our sixth-graders become more aware of the options they have when bullying does take place.

"I Should Have Stood Up for Myself."

Growing up, I had two really good friends who lived in my neighborhood. We would do everything together during the summer. We rode bikes all over town, even had lemonade stands when we were younger, and hung out almost every day. I remember one day my two friends were hanging out together and I joined them a little bit later. We were trying to decide what we wanted to do that day. I remember giving a couple of suggestions and they both turned them down. Then, one of my friends said, "I know what we can do! Let's sit in a circle and go around and tell each other what we don't like about each other." My other friend quickly agreed to this little game. I felt very uncomfortable with it, but I was outnumbered.

I'm not sure if this was something they had planned before I got there that day or if it had to do with the fact that I was a little too uncomfortable to say much, but it turned into a bit of time where they were both just telling me really mean things that they didn't like about me. They told me things like I needed to lose weight, that I wore ugly boy clothes, that boys didn't like me because I wasn't pretty enough, etc. I don't really remember how this "game" ended but I think I probably just ended up walking back to my house after feeling bad enough.

DOI: 10.4324/9781003368779-16

Looking back, I know I should have stood up for myself and not allowed that to happen, but it was really difficult for me to say something to my best friends. I was worried that if I didn't play the game they wanted to play that they would stop being friends with me. I was really shy and didn't like confrontation, so the thought of having to try and make new friends was really scary. I don't think I ever really told them just how terrible that game felt to me.

I wish I could say I am more comfortable with standing up for myself, but it's still something I struggle with as an adult. It's hard to know when to stand up for what you think is right (especially when speaking with your boss or teacher) and when to just "be the bigger person" and leave the situation alone and not say anything. I am telling you this story because I think it's important to learn at a young age that sometimes it's okay to speak your mind and let someone know that you are uncomfortable by their actions. You deserve to be treated with respect, especially by your friends! You don't have to stay in any kind of relationship where you aren't treated with respect. Even if finding new friends seems scary, it will probably be better in the long run. I'm wondering if we could practice now: What could I have said to those "friends" back then when they were saying those mean things to me?

The Bully Closest to You

Growing up, I had a cousin who lived in a town near me. Believe it or not, her name was Kate (like mine) and we were born just five days apart! Almost like twins! We spent a lot of time together as kids and I always thought of her as one of my best friends. We would be with each other for all our family gatherings and we would have sleepovers together and spend a lot of time alone together. I did not have any other cousins who were our age and she was one of my first friends. Well, Kate and I mostly got along. But we were really different from one another. Kate was always more outgoing and not afraid to get what she wanted. I admired her for always knowing what she wanted and how she felt, and I didn't feel like I always knew that.

As we were getting older, I started noticing some things about our relationship. Kate was really assertive and controlling, and really liked things her way. I was always more of a shy kid and tended to go with the flow. As we were getting to the end of elementary school, I would find myself leaving her house and feeling so sad and weird. She would force me to do things I did not want to do, made really rude comments to me, and was so controlling. She was always bossing me around and eventually it started getting to me. I felt like the worst friend and the worst cousin because I did not want to hang out with her anymore. I did not want to create drama within the family and make a scene because I knew it would upset her and she would make a huge deal if I stood up to her. Every time I would try to stand up for myself, she was become so upset and turn it back on me to make me feel bad for her. I honestly did not know what to do at the time and felt really hopeless about the situation.

Eventually, as we got to middle school, we started hanging out with our own groups and did not spend as much time together, except at family events and sleepovers. We still saw each other a fair amount, but I was not wanting to hang out with her because of the way she made me feel. Eventually, I really did stop hanging out with her and we weren't on the best terms. One day, in probably eighth grade, I started getting these nasty texts from a random phone number. They said things like "no one will ever think you're cute because you are ugly" and other messages like that. I was so hurt that someone would send those texts to me and cried to my mom for hours. Eventually, I figured out it was Kate. I was so upset that she said those things to me.

Why am I telling you all this story? I remember hearing about bullies as a younger person and thinking that a bully was someone that everyone knew was a bully. I came to realize, though, that a lot of the times a bully can be one of the people closest to you. I never thought of my cousin as a bully until I was able to realize all of the hurt that she caused me. I realized that she actually wasn't being a good friend to me at all. Not only did she say some mean things to me over the years, but I think she really took my voice away. I was so afraid to speak up for myself and voice my opinions, something I am honestly still working on. I learned from this experience that I would not let anyone treat me or others around me that way again. I'm hoping we can talk about the ways we deal with bullies who might be people closest to us, like friends and family members.

I Wish I Had Stood Up For Her

Today, I'm going to share a story with you that is kind of hard to share, because I feel vulnerable sharing about some decisions I made when I was younger. I really appreciated last week how you all listened to my story, and today I only want to share my story if I know I'll be listened to and not be made fun of, so can you give me a thumbs up if you agree to listen to my story with respect, without interruptions, and definitely no teasing!

During my fourth grade year, I was in a new school, as I had just moved to Arizona. I was beginning to make friends with the other quiet people, learning that just because the loud and popular people weren't friends with me didn't mean I couldn't make friends with other people that might be more like me. I became friends with a girl named Erica, one of my two friends that year. Erica was quiet, shy, and pretty awkward around other people. Erica had told me that her family didn't have much money, and because of this, she didn't have many good clothes she could wear to school. She also told me she frequently was bullied for the clothes she wore.

One day, Erica was wearing the same outfit she had worn all week – sneakers, jeans, and a hoodie covering a shirt that did not meet the school's dress code. We were standing in the hallway in line waiting to go to our next class when Anna and Cindy, the popular girls of fourth grade, walked up to Erica, beginning to tease her about her clothes and what she was wearing. I was standing right behind Erica, but chose not to say anything, even though Erica was visibly upset. Before Anna and Cindy walked away, they pulled Erica's hoodie zipper down all the way, breaking the zipper with force so Erica wouldn't be able to zip her hoodie back up, saying "oh, I guess you won't meet dress code anymore," then laughed and walked away. Erica's face showed embarrassment and she looked to be on the verge of tears.

I wish I had stood up for her and said something to Anna and Cindy, or even had the right words to say to Erica to let her know I had her back. Instead, I did nothing, not wanting the girls to start to bully me. Erica eventually was written up for not meeting dress code and sent home to change, causing her to feel even more alone and embarrassed. I think Erica could have really used a friend to tell Anna and Cindy that what they were doing was mean, and maybe Erica would have had a better day knowing she wasn't alone.

I Laughed and Encouraged Him

My story comes from my first year in high school. I was beginning to find larger groups of friends that I had more in common with, but I still struggled with wanting to be accepted by the popular kids, craving their attention and approval. In my freshman year, I had a crush on a boy named Kim, who was sort of popular, really funny, and would often get in trouble with teachers for his behavior in class. He ended up liking me back, which was a really new feeling for me because no one had ever liked me like that before. I wanted to continue to be liked by him and his friends, as I finally felt like I sort of belonged. However, I quickly learned that Kim and his friend group would often pick on a girl named Mia. Mia was regularly made fun of for having long, untamed, fiery red curls that made her stand out from everyone else. Mia tried to ignore people when they'd bully her, but would also respond to bullies with loud and aggressive responses to try to protect herself, only to be made fun of more.

Kim and I sat next to each other in English class, often giggling together, drawing on our shoes, and not really paying attention to what was being taught. One day, Mia was sitting at the desk in front of Kim, and her long hair was lying on Kim's desk. He began to play with it, tossing it around, and coloring on it with a marker. I was laughing, which continued to encourage his behavior. It then became clear to me that Kim had taken scissors out of his backpack, planning to cut off a small lock of Mia's hair. I felt weird about it, because Mia was on my volleyball team and I knew she didn't like it when people would pick on her. But I liked Kim and he liked me, so I didn't want to tell him not to do it. Instead, I laughed and encouraged him. He snipped about 3 inches off one of Mia's curls, then showed her. I watched her face turn pale, and her eyes well up with tears, feeling embarrassed and mad without finding the right response. I immediately felt guilty, because I had participated in an action that was really mean, with hopes that it would cause Kim to like me more. Things like this continued in my freshman year, and I continued to not say anything, going along with Kim's "funny" mean actions, laughing them off as jokes. I never said anything to him, but slowly withdrew from him and his group of friends my second year of high school, eventually finding a group of friends that were actually funny without needing to make fun or hurt people to have funny jokes to tell.

The reason I'm telling you this is because I think it's important to know that bullies can look very different, and can sometimes be hard to know how to identify them, especially if it's a friend who is the one being mean. I'm also telling you these stories because I wished I had confidence to stand up for others when I knew what was happening was wrong. I lacked understanding of what a bully could look like, and in the last story, I was a bully myself. In each of these cases, I remember a tiny voice in my head, a strange and weird feeling, telling me that something was wrong, that what was happening was really mean, but in both these cases, I prioritized the opinions of people who were mean over acknowledging when someone's actions were actually hurting someone. I had felt lonely and without friends so often, but didn't understand that friends could come from anywhere, not just from the groups of people who made themselves noticeable because of the mean things they did.

"I Actually Love Her Outfit."

When I was in sixth grade, I was struggling with making friends. I had some friends from outside of school from theater and summer camp, but I didn't have many friends in school itself. I had always loved to dance, and decided to try out for the cheerleading team. I was pretty shy, but I thought it might be fun to do the routines. Some of the cheerleaders found out that I was trying out and started talking to me. They were very popular, and they began inviting me to eat lunch with them and asking me to hang out with them in other classes.

Before tryouts, a friend I had from theater, Marina, transferred into my school. I was super excited, but then I heard the popular girls making fun of her. They made fun of her appearance, clothes, and hobbies. Part of me wanted to stand up and tell them how awesome I thought she was, but I had worked so hard to try to fit in with these new "friends." Instead, I laughed along with them.

One day we were sitting behind Marina in the gym, and one of the popular girls started to talk about her appearance again. Marina turned around and looked at me. I froze at first but then realized that I wasn't being myself with the popular girls. Many of the things that they were making fun of Marina for (her love for theater, dressing differently, etc.) were things I loved about Marina and things I also liked myself. At that moment I looked at the popular girls and said, "I actually love her outfit and y'all should stop being so mean." I actually said something worse than that!

Marina smiled at me and I stepped down from the popular students to sit by her. Days later I began getting bullied along with Marina, and I didn't make the cheerleading team. The popular students made fun of our clothes, hobbies, etc. It was hard some days but it was worth it many other times because I had a true friend who wasn't scared to be herself. She made me braver. Marina and I are still best friends to this day. I'm telling you this story because although I know it can be hard to stand up against bullies, and you may lose certain things, I can promise you that you will feel better about it in the long run, like I do.

"I Was Proud to Have a Gay Parent."

When I was in fifth grade, I had a lot of friends at my elementary school. I felt lucky that a lot of those friends were going to the same middle school as me. I was so excited to start sixth grade and be able to reinvent myself as a big kid. I did have one worry: My big sister, Melissa, would be an eighth grader at my new school. My sister and I have a better relationship now, but when we were 11 and 14, we did not get along. I couldn't do anything right, and she always made fun of me and hurt my feelings. When her friends were around, they would also make fun of me. They would say that I had huge front teeth that needed to be filed down, that I had frizzy hair that needed to be straightened, and they would call me my least favorite word: Annoying!

Sharing middle school with her was really hard sometimes. I had lots of friends and loved my classes, especially dance class, where I was allowed to join the seventh-grade level and meet new friends a year above me who knew the middle school ropes. Everything was great, except for Melissa and her friends, who would ignore me in the hallway and then be disgusted that they had to take the bus home with me. Melissa would whisper with her friends then they would all laugh about my outfits.

Our school put on two dance recitals every year. As the Winter dance recital approached, I was getting so eager to have my family see me perform. I was really proud of myself for getting to dance with the older kids, and I even had a solo in the show. A couple of weeks before the show, my sister came into my room very angry. She told me I was going to be a loser, and everyone was going to hate us because we were freaks. With tears in her eyes, she told me to keep my mouth shut about our mom or she would beat me up. She was mad because I had been telling my dance class about who from our family was going to come to the show. I told them about my dad and his girlfriend, our family friends, my aunt, uncle and cousins, and my mom and her girlfriend. My mom and dad divorced when I was young, and it was a little later that she told me and Melissa that she was gay and introduced us to her girlfriend, Sheri. I loved Sheri and became best friends with her daughter who was my age and loved everything I loved. I was proud to have a gay parent. We marched in the PRIDE parade every year, and it felt good to have a community of unique people and family members. My sister did not feel the same way and was embarrassed, thinking that everyone at our school would hate us if they knew.

Over the next weeks I felt like I was holding onto a huge secret. I felt like my whole life and family were a big, bad secret. Melissa's shame spread to me and I became very quiet and afraid. I wasn't even excited to dance in the recital anymore. I cried every day, worried that Melissa would find out that I told people our mom was gay. I felt sick on the day of the recital. I smiled on stage, but I wasn't happy inside. After the show, I came out from backstage to find my family waiting for us. I saw my mom and Sheri holding hands, her daughter waving me over with flowers in her hand. My body shook with fear, and I felt like I couldn't breathe. I looked around and no one was looking at us, or if they were, they just smiled and waved and said "Great job, Ellie!". Not noticing, or caring, that my mom had a girlfriend. I asked my mom where Melissa was, and found out that she decided to stay home. For the first time in weeks, I took a sigh of relief, but was also sad that she didn't want to see me dance.

I'm telling you this story because sometimes when we think of bullying, we don't think about it coming from someone in our family. When I thought about my experience with bullying, it was really hard for me to sit with the fact that my biggest bully was my big sister. I know now that it was my sister who was really struggling. It was our older cousin who told my sister that we should be ashamed of my mom, and my sister was very depressed. She was frustrated by how happy I was and jealous that I was able to fit into middle school so easily. It hadn't been that way for her in sixth grade. She was also really jealous of Sheri's daughter, and felt like she was being replaced as a sister. I learned about all of this years later, after Melissa had bullied me so badly we didn't talk to each other for about a year. When we started working on our sisterhood again during high school, I learned that behind my bully was another bully, and probably another one behind them. The important part is that the cycle ended with me. I wasn't afraid to be part of an LGBTQ family. I love them, and I love my big sister too.

"I Defined Myself."

When I was in upper middle school, I joined the swim team. This was a choice I made to have opportunities to connect more with my peers and have a healthy regiment in working out after school. Early on in my swim career, I turned out to be quite fast for just a beginner. I was fast enough that I had broken some senior's records in my events, which didn't please some of the more veteran swimmers too much. However, with my good races, I was gaining status on my team. I even received a nickname on the team: The Jew.

Yes, I am Jewish, and growing up in Nevada, I was an ethnic and religious minority. I took the nickname in stride. After all, I was being recognized and that was nice. I enjoyed the nickname at first, it felt empowering, I was fast, and people were excited for me to race. I know that most of the kids on the team meant only positive intentions with the name, though they clearly didn't realize how insulting it was to categorize someone like me by my ethnicity.

The name, however, had a negative snowball effect for some of my peers and how they would treat me. It seemed clear that some didn't want the name to be empowering for me. I discovered this over time through various microaggressions. One microaggression sticks out to me: One day, when I got to the locker room, a kid was really excited to tell me he had hidden coins throughout the locker room and wanted to "test me" and see if I could find them all in the short time we had before being expected at the pool. Their belief was I could sniff out the coins and find them all, which referenced two stereotypes about Jews: One about our noses and one about our relationship with money.

I'd like to say that I didn't feed into that specific microaggression, but I was still new. Instead of standing up for myself, I played along with the joke to avoid conflict or limit my chances of connecting with my peers. I played along, validating their stereotypes, and putting myself down in the process. I'm not upset with myself now that I did that then, because I know the pressure I was facing. But now that I am older and can look back on it all with a better perspective, I know that in the end, I found a way to silence my critics. By the end of my swim career, I was voted in to be team captain, and I had won my events at state helping our team become state champions. I earned a positive reputation with the team from my skills and determination. In the end, I did not let them use my ethnicity to define me and to be tokenized. Instead, I defined myself using my skills as a swimmer and good teammate.

"Lorraine! Lorraine! Lorraine!"

I'm going to tell you guys a personal story. It's a story from when I was in the sixth grade and something I'm not proud of. Even though I'm a little embarrassed to share this, I do it so that maybe you guys can learn from my mistake. Are you ready? Okay, here it is.

Like I said I was in the sixth grade. I lived in a neighborhood where several of us had the same bus stop. Every day, before the bus came, I went to my friend Lorraine's house. I really enjoyed going to her house! She came from a large Greek family and her mom was always so gracious to me and told me how sweet I was. They seemed to always have fresh baked pita bread and her mom would insist on sharing a bag for me to take home to my family. It was so delicious and warm, I gratefully accepted. I remember being intrigued with Lorraine's home because she didn't have many things to play with. In fact, her room was quite barren and her bed was always made; unlike mine. We were never allowed to play in her room. Instead, she was entertained by my amazing head-standing abilities in her basement. I kind of enjoyed being a show-off for her and being her entertainer.

Many mornings were spent with me on my head while she watched and timed me; challenging me to stay upside down until the bus was coming. Lorraine was a super nice, kind, quiet, and friendly girl. Though she was the type of friend that was my neighborhood, and bus friend, she was not so much my school friend.

When the bus dropped us off at school, we would go our separate ways. I'm actually not sure who her friends were but I had other friends I would run off to.

On one particular Friday, I was getting ready to have my very best friend, Leigha, come home on the bus with me to spend the night. I was feeling super excited about this. It was unusual for my mom to let me have a friend spend the night for a sleepover. Also, for her to come home on the bus with me felt really, really special. I was so excited I could barely focus all day in school! On the bus ride home, I remember getting on with Leigha and finding that the bus was already pretty full. We found two open spaces that were across the aisle from each other and grabbed them. They happened to be just behind where Lorraine was sitting. I'm not sure what exactly I was thinking, but this is where the story gets embarrassing. I began chanting Lorraine's name. Not in a cheering on, positive way, but in somewhat of a taunting manner: "Lorraine! Lorraine! Lorraine!" This got the attention of the people surrounding and they started laughing. Lorraine on the other hand was not acknowledging it. The chanting was getting attention and for some reason I thought it was fun. I then began using rhymes with her name: Florraine, Klorraine, Slorraine! The one that stuck was Slorraine. "Lorraine Slorraine! Lorraine Slorraine! Slorraine! Slorraine!" A few others started joining in my chant. Lorraine was not seeming to react. She kept staring straight ahead. She never even turned around to look at me. When we arrived to our stop Lorraine got off the bus first. As Leigha and I started walking up my street I yelled at Lorraine, her back to me, "Bye, Slorraine!" and laughed. When my friend and I got to my house we immediately dropped our book bags and headed outside to play. We probably weren't outside for more than ten minutes before my mom came out to us with a disappointed look on her face. She said Lorraine's mom had just called her because her daughter was in tears. Lorraine's mom told my mom that she couldn't believe I would hurt her daughter so badly.

And so that is my story. A story I'm not proud of, but one that I hope I learned from. I hope I learned that it is possible for anyone, even me, to be the bully. That I have the power to exclude, or include, others. That I have the power to hurt others, or make them feel good. I hope that by sharing it with you, you can learn from it too. One thing I hope we can talk about is, under what conditions do we bully others? Why do you think I was picking on Lorraine on the bus that day?

"Everyone in the School Was Completely Avoiding Sara."

I have many memories of junior high school, but I have one in particular that stands out to me crystal clear. I was in the sixth grade. I went to a very small school. My entire sixth-grade class had about 16 students in it. We all knew each other from kindergarten and it was really hard to constantly fit in with what was cool. I had two friends named Lexia and Kali and they were easily the two most popular girls in our class. Probably, in the whole school. I had known them both my whole life and frequently found myself in their friend group. I am not sure why they were considered so popular. They were both really pretty with long beautiful hair. They also had the newest clothes and the most stylish everything. They weren't, however, particularly kind.

I remember one day in particular. We were in the cafeteria. We had such a small Jr. High that there was only one lunch period and we all had to sit in alphabetic order. This never bothered me much because both Lexia and Kali sat at my table since our names were close in order. On this particular day, they were both telling us all a shocking piece of news. They said a girl in my class, Saria, had a disgusting disease called scabies. Scabies is an infestation of skin mites. They bite you and burrow down into your skin and cause itchiness and an angry rash. One of the worse parts is that scabies is highly contagious. That means that you can get it by just touching the other person. Quickly everyone in the school was completely avoiding Saria.

This wasn't the first time Saria had been the focus of teasing and gossip in our school. Saria's family didn't have a lot of money. She often came to school in the same clothes that were often dirty or smelly. This did not help her fit in with her class. Saria was also in a separate class for most of the day and went to special education classes. Saria only joined the rest of the class for a few times during the day, including lunch and recess.

When Lexia and Kali were telling everyone that Saria had this awful infection, I felt sick to my stomach. They didn't seem to have any real reason to believe that this was true. I had a strong suspicion that it was a lie. But I didn't want to confront them. I had been working for years to be in the popular crowd and I definitely wasn't going to lose my status over a girl that I didn't know or care much about. So, I stayed quiet. I did not, however, spread the lie myself. I did not participate in the conversation. I just ate my lunch and waited for it to end.

Pretty soon the teachers heard about the rumor and told everyone that it was completely untrue. People were quickly questioned to see where the rumor had begun. I was in social studies class when I was called into the Principal's office. I was terrified. I knew if I got into trouble at school I would be punished at home. When I got to in to see the Principal, Mrs. Caston, I immediately confessed my innocence. I said that I didn't start the rumor. That I didn't even participate in the conversations. I remember she looked at me for a moment and was quiet. It felt like hours. When she did speak, I remember her sighing and looking sad. She said she knew I did not start the rumor, but she wondered why I did not stand up for Saria and say that the rumors were untrue. She said that she really expected me to speak up for someone like Saria, and that she was disappointed that I hadn't. With that she sent me back to class.

The reason I am telling you this is because, to this day, I can remember how devastated I felt. I knew I should have spoken up for Saria but I was afraid to. I had let my fear of losing popularity keep me from doing what I knew deep down was the right thing to do. I had a chance to be a friend, an ally, a decent classmate, and I failed. I saw bullying happen and I remained silent. I hope we can talk about how tough it is to step in from the bystander role, but also how important it is and how we can do it in so many ways.

"What, You Trying to Copy Me Now?"

When I was in middle school, I remember there was a group of older Latina girls. They were all a year older than I was and where I lived, there weren't many Hispanic students like me in my school. I remember always trying to hang out with them, fit in by wearing similar clothes, talking in a similar way and trying to basically act like they did in school. I knew that they carried weight in the school, because others also dressed like they did and were friends with a lot of people it seemed like. I'm not sure a lot of people outside of their group liked them because they often made fun of other people, mocked them, and teased them. Including me.

After my sixth grade year and starting seventh grade, they were on top of the school because they were eighth graders now. I was still just another kid beneath them, a seventh grader. One day I remember wearing a skirt, tennis shoes, and a necklace that had some cherries on them. One of the girls in the group was Bianca and her "thing" was cherries. Cherries everything: From her clothes, pens, jewelry, shoelaces, really anything that she found with cherries on them, she had. So, this one day I came to school with the necklace on and she noticed. She came up to me and asked what I was doing. I was confused until she pointed to my necklace and said, "What, you trying to copy me now? How stupid. They don't look as good on you anyway. Whatever." As she walked away, I remember standing by my locker a little shocked, embarrassed, and unsure about what to do. I also remember this was not the first time she made fun of me for doing something that she had already done or worn before. I kept my necklace on for the day, but definitely didn't wear it again for a while.

One day a few weeks later, Bianca came up to me and said: "What, now you're not going to wear it because I said something?" and laughed at me. Again, I felt confused, embarrassed, and unsure of what to do. I was never good at comebacks.

The reason why I'm telling you this story is because when I was in middle school, I had a hard time standing up for myself, especially to older students who felt powerful. I knew that if I said the wrong thing or visibly got upset over it, it would be even worse with Bianca and her group teasing me. But a few weeks later I began to wear my necklace again and chose to keep some distance from people who were not kind to me and make friends who with others who didn't make fun of me. The teasing didn't stop, but it also didn't happen as often as it previously did, and by giving myself space to meet other people, I met one of my best friends who I still talk with today as an adult.

Finding Belonging
Strategic Story Examples

Overview

Belonging is a central and difficult issue for adolescents – and all of us! How can one find a sense of belonging and connectedness to others without compromising our own values? How can we navigate the strong pull to belong when the group we want to belong to turns out to not be kind to others outside that group? How can we be patient and careful in choosing who we want to belong to as well as clear and respectful when choosing not to belong to a particular group? These are the kinds of complex issues we try to help our sixth-graders unravel with stories like the ones in this section.

"Two Quality Friends Can Support You More Than Fifteen Can."

Belonging can be tough. For most of my childhood, especially in middle school, I thought it was very important to have a lot of friends. In the summer prior to me entering high school, I went to a residential summer camp. It was my first time ever going to a summer camp, for the whole summer! I was unsure of how it was going to go. When I arrived, I was assigned to a bunk in a dorm room on the second floor. There were 52 students, all boys, on that floor, including myself. The first few days at the camp went really well. I became part of a large group of friends, about 12 or 13 of us. I also had two other friends, Kevin and Tal, who were slightly older than me at the time.

Every day after our morning school-related activities, we would all get together and hang out in each other's dorm rooms. Over the course of the first two weeks of the camp, I was somehow given the nickname "Aladdin" because I was the only brown-skinned kid in the group. I want to say that throughout the course of building relationships with them, I had not really considered my or their race or ethnicity. However, I did notice cultural differences between me and the larger group. Musical tastes, clothing choices, and style of humor, for example. I also noticed that they sustained their friendships with each other through making fun of each other. Like calling each other names such as "Midget," and "Baldy" to

DOI: 10.4324/9781003368779-17

name just a few. After a few more days at camp, my initial nickname of "Aladdin" somehow changed to "Bingi" because I was a "dirty Indian kid," or so they said jokingly. At first, I tried to play along with this nickname because I felt that being a part of a large group of friends was essential. I told myself, "Well, everyone is getting made of fun of so it's all right." The humor continued throughout our daily walks to classes, lunchtime, and other free periods.

Over a month into the camp, I found myself emotionally and mentally drained. Everyone else seemed to be doing fine. I felt like the odd man out, and the humor became harsher and harsher. One night, while we were all hanging out in the dorms, we started to talk about our classes. The conversation swiftly changed to making fun of teachers and each other. One of the boys looked at me and said, "You must be smart because you're Indian, right?" I had taken enough, I walked out of the room towards my own dorm room. I was thinking I could just brush it off again, but instead I broke down in my room. As a boy, showing emotions like crying may be seen negatively. So, I left the dorm for privacy, but somehow bumped into Kevin and Tal, my friends. They saw how upset I was and took me over to their dorm. I opened up about everything that was happening over the course of the first month of the camp. Both of them really supported me and sat with me for a few hours talking about how difficult friendships and bullying within friendships can be. They supported me right there and told me they would be there for me for the rest of camp.

The reason I'm telling you this story is that it may seem that having lots of friends is important. However, I want to push back on this way of thinking and tell all of you that the quality of those friendships is more important than the quantity of friends we have. In hindsight, I was friendly to people who did not earn my trust and in fact bullied me. I also overlooked some potential friends because I valued being in large groups more. Now I know that two quality friends can support you more than 15 can.

"I Found Community and a Sense of Belonging."

Today I will be telling you a story about my experience of how I found a sense of belonging in a community. I grew up in a small town and when I look back on my middle-school experience, I remember more positive experiences rather than negative experiences. However, when I was in elementary school, I started Girl Scouts. I remember being very excited but also nervous to get the opportunity to make new friends and to take part in projects that would help my community. I belonged to the same Girl Scout troop for many years. Being a part of this troop gave me many positive experiences, but as we got older, the girls that had always been in my troop began to quit one by one because they thought that Girl Scouts were childish, embarrassing, and uncool. Eventually, there were only four of us left in the group by the time we got into eighth grade. We would usually meet after school at the church right next to our middle school and, as we walked over there, we started getting teased and bullied for going to Girl Scouts: "Ooh, the babies are going to their baby Girl Scout group." They called us names, made faces at us, and rolled their eyes as walked by.

Being bullied for being a part of the Girl Scout troop made us feel embarrassed and even question whether we wanted to stay in the Girl Scouts. But we talked about it and decided that we liked it, that it was important to us, and that we wanted to stay in it. We decided not to talk about being a part of this group at school, and if we did talk about it, we would use the code word "cookies" to know what we were talking about. Being a part of the Girl Scout troop gave me access to many positive and different opportunities that I would otherwise not have been able to experience. I gained experiences like learning about different cultures, traveling to new places, going camping, learning important values, and learning important ways to give back to my community. I found community and a sense of belonging and that was a good thing.

The reason I am telling you this story is because sometimes you can get teased or bullied by others for belonging to a specific kind of community or group that might be seen as uncool, even if it's a good thing. But I'm really glad I didn't leave that group because I was teased for it. I didn't change my values or sacrifice the things that were important to me just because some other kids thought the Girl Scouts were embarrassing. I'm really glad I didn't miss out on gaining cherished experiences and memories that I still think about to this day.

"I Joined the Band."

When I was in sixth grade, I felt like I didn't have much of a social center. I felt like I was a bit of a social butterfly, floating between groups. Although I generally had a positive experience with my first year of middle school, I felt like I was going through the motions, socially. I drifted from group to group, altering my style and personality sometimes to fit in, but many groups didn't fit right. I think I was feeling a little lost after having a closer connection with my elementary school friends where I was in only one classroom with the same students every day.

Then in seventh grade I joined the band. Although it took me some time to realize it, I felt more comfortable in the band than I did in many of my other classes. The focus on creativity helped me feel like I could be myself and explore my interests in music, which made me feel at ease. The band had an element of healthy competition and support. For example, we had competitions for who could get First Chair, as well as solo competitions. Looking back, this gave me incentive to practice and helped me learn to accept both failure and success, and support others in the spirit of camaraderie. I still acted in ways that would allow me to "fit in" with the group, but it came much easier and I felt fulfilled.

Being part of a band gave me an opportunity to meet others from backgrounds other than my elementary school and expand my horizons socially. Because of the band, I could take pride in my hobby and connect with my friends over a common interest. I felt empowered and lucky that I could travel with my friends because of my interest in music. I was able to gain access to experiences that I wouldn't have had otherwise, like traveling with the band to competitions and festivals, and even playing at Disneyland, where we got to learn how Walt Disney Studios recorded bands and orchestras for their movies.

I'm telling you this story because I want you to see how being part of a group with a common interest can make you feel a greater sense of belonging and also help develop your uniqueness, a theme we'll be discussing further next week. To be honest, when I was first thinking about joining the band way back then, I was worried that joining a band would make me seem uncool. Truthfully, I don't remember if I got any negative comments about it. Maybe there were a few here and there. But imagine what I would have missed out on if I had listened to that fear! It's often worth taking the risk of engaging in something you care about: When you find others who also care, the support can help develop your involvement with the community and also develop your unique interests, be it with a religious group, music ensemble, art class, or sports team.

"I Gave in and Followed Her at Lunch."

Just like last week, I want to make sure that we are all ready for my story. Are you ready to listen without laughing or talking over me? Okay, thank you everyone. I had a big friend group in middle school, but when we got into high school, we all went our separate ways. We grew apart because we all started to like different things and some people started getting boyfriends and girlfriends. Because of that, it happened that just Rochelle and I hung out after a while. We were best friends and mostly relied on each other for everything. Unfortunately, when we turned 15, Rochelle's dad died of cancer. She was very sad about it and her behavior changed. She was doing things that hurt herself and others because she had a hard time dealing with the loss of her father.

Once, when we were eating lunch together, the school resource officer handcuffed her and took her away. It was sad and scary because I didn't know what to do or what to say to Rochelle. And that was the last time I saw her for five years. When Rochelle left, I was all alone, which was my greatest fear back then. I used to watch the clock in class, dreading break and lunch because I would have to find somewhere to hide.

One day, I was sitting out on the grass of our baseball field by myself, far away from the lunch area. I heard footsteps approaching from behind me. I turned around and discovered it was my sister. My sister was a little younger than me and we weren't very close at this time. She was a freshman in high school. We were also going through our own family problems at home and both of us avoided being home. Every week and weekend, we were staying at friend's or other family member's house. So, in a way, my sister felt like a stranger to me.

She sat down next to me and asked why I was sitting alone. I told her I didn't have anyone to hang out with since Rochelle was kicked out of school. She said that I could hang out with her and her friends if I wanted. I said no. They were younger than me and I didn't want to seem weird.

The next day, though, I gave in and followed her at lunch. Even though I didn't have much in common with my sister's friends, they included me and I enjoyed having people to talk to again. But even more important was I got to talk with my sister which is something I hadn't done in a while. We talked about everything: our problems, our crushes, our dreams of getting out of our small town. I hadn't ever thought about asking her about her life. She told me how much she hated being home with all of our family problems. And sometimes she felt alone, even though she had friends.

Even though my sister and I fought a lot growing up, her act of kindness and care back then changed how I looked at her and our relationship. She helped me in a time of need and accepted me even when I rejected her offer to hang out. I'm telling this story because sometimes we find ourselves alone. And it's good to be alone sometimes, that is something I've learned to LOVE as an adult. But other times we want friendship and companionship and that's okay. There may be times in your life where you find out you belong with someone or a group of people that you hadn't considered before. I hope all of you give yourself and other people a chance to create those connections, too.

"I Wrote a Letter to All My Close Friends."

This is a story from middle school. This story is something that happened to me and my family that was really difficult. You or someone you know may be able to relate to this story. When I was in sixth grade my mom was diagnosed with cancer. When she was diagnosed with cancer, the doctor told our family she only had two years to live. This broke my heart and I was so scared to lose my mom.

Almost every day, I would leave one of my classes, go to the front office and call my mom. We talked about random little things, like what I was going to eat for lunch or what I was doing in school. I really just wanted to hear her voice. Going and talking to her made me feel better because I was so worried and anxious about losing her and couldn't imagine my life without her. A big part of this story is that I never talked to any of my friends about this. Most of them knew that my mom had cancer but I never told them myself. I think I was worried that if I talked about it with my friends it would feel "too real" or that I would cry and couldn't stop (this is something I didn't want to do in front of my friends).

Leaving class and talking with my mom lasted for a couple of years. Sometimes I wouldn't go on school trips or go to sleepovers with my friends because I didn't want to leave her or I was afraid something might happen to her when I was gone. I didn't lose any friends but I felt I was hiding something from them. This didn't feel very good or honest.

After she died, I wrote a letter to all my close friends explaining what it was like to experience living with a sick parent and why sometimes I would leave class, not spend as much time with them, or not do other things. When they received the letter all my friends responded with so much love and understanding. Most of them said to me that they knew all of that but appreciated the letter.

I wanted to share this story with you all because I think it is really important to talk to people, especially people who care about you, like your friends, when you are experiencing hard and scary things. All my friends knew I was going through this yet I never talked to them about it. Looking back, I wish I would have been more open about my emotions. I think it would have been hard and taken a lot of courage to talk about what I was feeling. Sharing these feelings probably would have made me feel less alone and less scared to lose my mom because I would have felt connected with all my friends.

"Then She Said That She Forgave Me."

When I was in middle school, the most important thing to me was fitting in. I used to beg my parents to buy me designer jeans, Abercrombie & Fitch sweatshirts, and Uggs – like the ones Paris Hilton used to wear. Being in middle school felt competitive to me – if you had the "right" clothes, sat at the "right" table, and were invited to the "cool" parties, then you won and the person who wasn't invited lost. At the school I went to, there were definitely "cool" kids and then everyone else; I was on the edge of the "cool" kids. Most of the time, I was one of them, but I wasn't the coolest of the cool kids. As a result, it left me feeling competitive and fearful that somebody else would show up and take my spot. I spent a lot of my time feeling like I wasn't quite enough, and was so scared of what would happen if everyone else suddenly decided they didn't like me. It really felt like that would be the worst thing in the world. At my core, I was a nice person though. I wanted people to be happy around me and I wanted to relax and not have to care so much about what everyone thought.

In sixth grade, I had three classes with the same group of kids. A lot of the "cool" girls were in this group, and I really wanted them to like me. There was also another girl trying hard to be "cool." Her name was Debonair, but all of the girls in the cool group had decided that they didn't like her. Debonair was a little bit louder than everyone else, and a little bit more excitable. Sometimes she would get excited about things that nobody else was, or she would make a loud comment about something that was a little bit personal to somebody else. Once she realized that the girls in this group were starting to roll their eyes at her, or exclude her from things, or make jokes about her, she started trying harder and harder to be liked. The harder she tried, the more people seemed put off by her.

Debonair and I were friends from elementary school and I liked her. Often, we would end up partnered with each other in class. In fact, we were supposed to go on a trip together to Europe with a few other people from our school that summer. Because I was trying so hard to fit in, once I noticed that the cool girls weren't liking her, I started to think less of her too. One day, I was having a sleepover with another girl from the cool group, and she was teasing me for being friends with Debonair. We decided to call Debonair and pretend that the two of us had just gotten into a fight. We didn't tell Debonair that the other one was in the room, and then got Debonair to talk negatively about the other person. We then called Debonair together and told her she was mean and that we didn't like her anymore for what she said about both of us. Debonair started crying, said she was so confused, and that she did like us. We hung up and then told a couple of our other friends about what she said, which made them like her less.

When I got home from the sleepover, I started feeling more and more guilty about what we had done. I was eating dinner with my parents that night and blurted out everything that my friend and I had just done to Debonair. My parents were furious that I had treated somebody else like that, and were disappointed in me for being a mean girl and bullying Debonair. As a consequence, aside from being grounded from the phone and social events, my mother asked Debonair's mother if Debonair was comfortable with me coming over to apologize. My mom drove me to her house, and I sat across from Debonair and her mom and apologized for what I'd done. It was very humbling and Debonair was crying because I'd violated her trust and made her feel bad about herself. My mom then asked Debonair if she felt comfortable with me going on the school trip to Europe. My mom was clear that Debonair deserved to have a good time on the trip, and if my being there would take away from her ability to have fun, it was absolutely fine to have me stay at home. Debonair thought about it for a minute, and then she said that she forgave me because she knew what it was like to try to fit in, and that she thought it would still be okay with her if I came on the trip to Europe too.

I'll never forget that moment because Debonair taught me what it was like to forgive somebody who hurts you. Her big heart and ability to give me a second chance made me want to be a better friend. We had a great time together in Europe that summer. I guess I'm telling you this story because I know that we all make mistakes in our relationships. But the important thing is to be willing to move toward repair, to try and make things better. It's also important to pay attention to how much we each want to be "cool" and be careful not to do bad things in our effort to be part of the "in group," especially to those who are our friends.

"I Was Going to Change My Plans."

When I was a freshman in high school, my friends and I decided we would go in a group to prom. My high school was small, and it allowed all grades to attend prom. It was also common for people to go as a group or as a date, and it was not very common for people to attend prom stag or alone. My best friend, May, arranged for the two of us and six more of our friends to go together in her parent's

12 passenger van. We had been planning what we would do for almost a month. We were going to all meet at May's house, then head to dinner, and then to the prom. Everyone in the group was excited about our plans.

One morning, my friend Solomon came up to me. He told me that he wanted to attend prom but had not found anyone to go with him. He also shared that he was not comfortable attending prom alone. I explained that I already had plans and was going to the dance with our friends from middle school. After sharing this, I thought that maybe we could have Solomon come with us if I asked May. I figured it was not a big deal because we still had some space in the van. I also did not want to invite Solomon without talking to May first because she was planning everything. After a few days of thinking about my idea, May told me that although she and I were friends with Solomon, it was not a good idea for him to come with our group. She told me that there was just not enough space in the van for him. At first, I was relieved that I had not mentioned it to Solomon first, then I was upset because I thought my friends were mean for not wanting Solomon to come with us.

When I got home, I told my mom about what was going on and how it was bothering me. I told her that I kept picturing the look on Solomon's face when he told me how much he wanted to go to prom. The whole experience was not sitting well with me, and I started questioning my judgment of my friends. I also did not want to leave Solomon out, and I wanted him to come with us because I knew he was tons of fun and liked to dance. With the help of my mom, I decided that I was going to change my plans for prom.

The next day at school, I told May that I would no longer go with her and the group to prom. Then I found Solomon and asked if he wanted to go to prom with me and maybe some other friends that wanted to go but did not have a date or group to go with them. He said that sounded like fun, and we ended up finding two other friends, Cael and Tonia. The four of us had a good time. We still talk about that prom when we see each other. I am sharing this story because we all feel the need to belong to a group. It is also important to remember that our friends and classmates might also feel the need to belong. Sometimes we need to create a space to help others feel included.

"You Are Not Stealing This Necklace."

One Saturday when I was in sixth grade, two girls who were in the "cool" group, Mirium and Anna, invited me to go to the mall with them. The mall on a Saturday was "the place to be." When people at my middle school went to the mall it wasn't usually to buy clothes; it was simply a time to socialize and run into other people from school, get a pretzel or soda, and just walk around window-shopping. My mom also worked in the management department of the mall so I spent A LOT of time there – I knew every corner and hallway of that mall. So, there we were, shopping and going in and out of stores like American Eagle™,

Hollister™, Forever 21™, and Abercrombie™ and Fitch™. We were having a great time! I really felt accepted by these girls and liked that I belonged in this group. It was exciting to feel like I had been incorporated into the "cool kids" group.

We continued to shop and eventually found our way to JCPenney™. We were in Junior's section of the store looking at graphic t-shirts when Anna spotted a fixture with jewelry on it. It was costume jewelry made of colorful plastics, fake diamonds, and chunky beads. This style of jewelry was extremely popular when I was in high school. As we looked at the necklaces, one caught Anna's eye. She loved it and desperately wanted it. She looked at the price and quickly realized it was more expensive than the money she had brought with her. Suddenly, her posture changed, she began to slouch and whisper quietly, only loud enough for me and the other girls to hear: "I think I'm just going to take it," she said.

In that moment, I wasn't sure exactly what she meant until she began to describe her plans to steal the necklace from the store. Quickly, my face got hot, I began to sweat and get extremely nervous. I had never stolen anything before and it felt wrong. As Anna continued to explain her plan, I was trying to figure out a way to stop her from stealing. I knew stealing was wrong and I knew that the other girls knew stealing was wrong, but in that moment I had to decide if I wanted to go along with the plan just to fit in, or if I was going to stay true to my beliefs and listen to the signals my body was giving me and say "no" to stealing the necklace.

After what felt like a lifetime of silence, I spoke up: "You are not stealing this necklace," I said. "Why?" Anna asked. I began to explain that it was wrong and I was not comfortable with it. I also explained that my mom worked at the mall and that most people working in these stores knew who I was and there was no way I could be associated with shoplifting and get away with it. It really came down to me not wanting to be a part of this plan because it was wrong.

After a lot of debate, Anna agreed to not steal the necklace. I can't be certain that she didn't go back another day and end up taking it, but in that moment, I knew that I had stood up for what was right and honest to me, even though it might have been at the expense of this "friendship." I really wanted to belong to this new group of friends, but I didn't want to belong so badly that I was willing to go against my beliefs.

Even following this Saturday at the mall, we were still friends but I limited our friendship to school settings and large groups of people at birthday parties. I never wanted to feel the way I felt on that Saturday at the mall ever again and I now knew the limitations of my friendship with Anna.

The reason I told you this story is because at some point in life, whether in middle school or later in life, you might be faced with a situation similar to mine: You may really want to belong to a new group of friends or community, but just because you really want to be accepted by that group doesn't mean you have to sacrifice who you are or the values that are important to you in order to prove you belong. For me, it was about learning what situations I felt comfortable belonging in (group hangouts/parties) and what situations I didn't (shopping at the mall). It's important to be able to stand up for yourself and stand up for what is right, even if it looks different from the actions of others around you.

"I Was Only Half."

When I started sixth grade, I was in a unique position because I had just moved into a different school district. So, instead of knowing at least some of the students, I knew absolutely no one. Part of me was utterly intimidated by the tasks of navigating a brand-new school building and making new friends. The other part of me was excited and kind of thrilled at the idea of reinventing who I was. In a way, it didn't matter who I was or how I acted in elementary school because no one knew me back then. Because of this, I was open to becoming friends with anyone. It didn't matter to me if they were super smart or super athletic because I wasn't committed to a certain identity.

Within the first couple weeks of sixth grade, a girl named Sabitra noticed that I am Vietnamese. Sabitra is also Vietnamese. We both had dark hair and dark eyes. We both have interesting sounding names – Sabitra's last name is Nguyen and she was often made fun of because of that. My Vietnamese name is Tong which people made fun of as well. Sometimes, it felt like it was me and Sabitra against the world because we were generally different than most of the other kids.

Sabitra and I were a great team. For our literature class, we were partners in a group project. We read a book called The Joy-Luck Club by Amy Tan, which is a story about Chinese women growing up in San Francisco. We created a big, beautiful book that talked about each character's story in The Joy-Luck Club. We used glitter glue, silky ribbon, and fancy textured paper to make the book look really special and unique. Inside, we described the struggles of these Asian women as they tried to find happiness in a culture that was radically different from their own. Our project was so good that we won an award. We were both so proud of ourselves for creating something so beautiful, and so meaningful to our identities and our shared community.

The thing is, this is where our friendship started to disintegrate. Something that I didn't tell you in the beginning was that Sabitra and I were only half Vietnamese. And, it turns out our other half really mattered to her. Sabitra was half Vietnamese and half Chinese. This meant that she is fully Asian. And me, I am half Vietnamese and half White, which means I'm only half Asian. So, while Sabitra was reading the book that we did a project on, she saw that she was more similar to the Chinese characters. And she thought that I was more similar to the mean, White characters that treated the Chinese women badly.

This changed everything. The things we originally had in common became different. We both had dark hair, but Sabitra's was black and mine was only dark brown. We both had dark eyes, but our eyes were different shapes. Soon, Sabitra found different friends that were more Asian than me. Sometimes they would make fun of me for not knowing how to speak Vietnamese anymore. They would say things in Vietnamese while I was around because they knew I didn't understand. They told me I couldn't be as smart as them because I was "only half." And if I scored better than them on a test, it was because I was lucky. I guess I learned that in some cases, I'm just not Asian enough.

The reason I'm telling you this story is because belonging to a certain group of people can be both really empowering and also difficult. You can have a real sense of belonging and friendship because you have a lot of things in common. At the same time, you may find that there are ways in which you are different from those in that community. I think it is really important to find a group to belong to that accepts all of you, even the ways in which you are different.

"I Realized I Would Have to Choose."

Today I'm going to tell you a story about community. This is a story from my time in middle school and how it shaped how I experienced high school. This is an important story to me, so I really appreciate your quiet attention. Remember that a few weeks ago I told you about what it was like for me to start middle school. I felt a lot of nervousness and fear in my body as I found my way to my classes at a new school. I walked to school alone and I walked home alone. You'll remember that it was a really difficult start for me because I felt so different. I only took a few classes at the middle school and the rest was taught to me by my parents at home because I was being homeschooled.

At the middle school I took a Spanish class, a humanities class, and a band. In each of these classes I was seen as the homeschooled kid, but eventually I started to fit in. I particularly started to feel at home in my band class. After a few weeks the rigid chairs started to feel comfortable as I played in harmony with my classmates. It was hard work to learn my instrument and talk to the other kids in the class, but I kept working at it to find ways to connect. I stayed in band for all three years of my middle school experience and I learned a lot about how to make music.

When I was in eighth grade, I had to start thinking about what I would do in high school. Throughout middle school I had been a part of band, but I had also played on a soccer team with friends from another school. I realized I would have to choose between band and soccer in high school. To be in band I had to also do marching band, which was at the same time as soccer. I talked with my mom about what I should do and she told me that I would have to figure out what I wanted to do for myself, but that she would support me either way. When I thought about making the decision, I felt the same nervousness in my stomach that I felt when I started middle school because it brought up the same question for me: How would I stay true to my own interests and still find a way to fit in?

After several weeks I came to the conclusion that I loved music and wanted to pursue that more than I wanted to pursue soccer. I don't know where I would be now if I hadn't made that decision. When I entered high school, I found a group of friends in band that I wouldn't have met otherwise. I played a lot of beautiful music and I was able to find a great community that would support me throughout my time in high school.

The reason I'm telling you this is because the struggle of finding a community and working to be a part of it can be worth it. Being a part of something bigger than myself has made me a better person. I learned how to work with others, how to encourage my friends, and I became more confident and comfortable as an individual. Every person can be a part of a community and most of us benefit from it, but we do have to choose which community. We can't all do the same things and sometimes we fit better in certain groups, so it is important to take your time in thinking about what is important to you and how you can contribute to others. I've found a lot of joy in being part of the different communities I chose and I hope you can do the same.

Being Unique

Strategic Story Examples

Overview

Along with belonging, we consider "being unique" as one of the two fundamental struggles of adolescent development. If my need to belong is too strong, where will there be room to stand my own ground as a unique individual? If my uniqueness is something that I am often criticized or even bullied for, how can I still find a way to appreciate and respect my own difference and unique qualities? Also, how can I allow trusted others to help me find and "own" what is unique about myself? These are the kinds of complex and thorny issues we work to address with this last set of strategic stories.

"I Learned That I Was Really Good at Math."

When I was in eighth grade, I learned that I was really good at math. I was placed into an advanced learner's class with the goal of learning enough math to be able to skip Algebra during my freshman year of high school. There was only one advanced math class for the entire eighth grade. I remember feeling super excited about my first day, even though we were already halfway through the school year when I got into the class.

On my first day, I was very nervous, but I knew that I could do it. When I got there, the only open seat was at the very front of the class. I recognized a few of the other students in the classroom, but nobody that I would consider a friend. The first few weeks I didn't really talk to anyone. I just paid attention to the teacher, Mr. Finders, and turned in my assignments on time. Sometimes I even turned them in ahead of time. Even though being in the advanced math class was starting to feel kind of lonely, I was still happy to be there.

My hard work must have paid off because, after about a month, Mr. Finders asked me to join the school's math league. I was so excited by that because it made me feel really smart! I happily agreed without even considering the time commitment. After I agreed, he told me to come to the next meeting the following Monday.

DOI: 10.4324/9781003368779-18

I was super nervous, but I felt pretty confident as I walked to Mr. Finders' classroom the next week for my first math league practice. That was before I opened the door and saw the other math league members: They were all in my advanced math class, and they were all boys. Most of them looked at me sideways, a couple even snickered. My nervousness quickly shifted to discomfort. This would turn out to be just the beginning of my problems: The math league boys clearly didn't like that there was a girl on their team.

Over the following weeks, the boys often reminded me how they felt about my being there. Saying things like "math isn't for girls" or "you'll never get a problem right at any of the meets!" Their unkind words made it hard for me to practice. As a result, I wasn't getting any questions right to get points for our team at any of the meets. I felt so bad about myself because I knew that I was proving them right.

One day, after a meet, I was visibly upset and I was ready to tell Mr. Finders that I wanted to quit. But before I could, Myron, one of the boys, came up to me as we were about to get on the bus. He told me not to listen to the other boys, and that math is for everyone. More than that, when we got on the bus, Myron told the other boys to lay off! It felt so great to have someone believe in me and support me. The next practice, the other boys didn't taunt me and I was able to pay attention. The following meet, I got a question right and scored some points for our team! I felt so accomplished.

I am telling you this story for a couple of reasons: First, I think it is really important to follow whatever skills or interests you have, even if it means you are different from the crowd and even if others don't support you. Second, I do also think it is super important to find people who can support you, like Myron did for me. Everyone needs support as they pursue their dreams! Who are some people who support you in your uniqueness?

"Justin Could Also Shoot."

In eighth grade, I was in a gym class that had begun a 2 on 2 basketball tournament. The goal of the game was to take turn shooting three pointers while the other team tried to distract and tip the ball in. There was a kid named Justin in my class who had some kind of learning disability. He was not in any of my other classes, and I would just see him during P.E. When it came time to choose teams for this tournament, many of the most athletic kids teamed up in hopes of winning it all. I wasn't known as a basketball player and so I didn't really link up with anybody right away. But Justin approached me and said that he knew me because he knew my younger sister, then he asked if I wanted to be teammates. I wasn't sure about this. The tournament was going to go on for a few days and I didn't want to get my butt kicked every match. But, since I didn't seem to have many options, I said, "Sure."

Surprisingly, we turned out to be pretty good. We had a strategy in place: Justin would distract the other team's shooters, putting his hand in their faces, jumping up and down, and doing everything but touching them. I would sit under the basket and try to tip-in the other team's missed shots for extra points. We started to win! Justin could also shoot, and as we began to play some of the better teams, we continued to win. We went all the way to the finals.

During our winning streak Justin got a lot of positive comments from our classmates, and we both began to make more friends. In the finals, we made it a very close game, but we were playing against the two best basketball players in the school. They ended up winning, but Justin and I were just excited with how far we made it. I was also excited to be able to make new friends, especially making new friends with Justin. He went into every game with a positive attitude, and even when we lost, he was gracious and grateful for how far we had gotten. I was grateful too, because I had learned something, and that's why I wanted to tell you this story. I learned that you could never tell what kind of unique talents a person might have unless you risk getting to know them. I also learned that a person like Justin should not be judged on one attribute like his learning disability. So, this is not so much a story about how I was unique, but how Justin taught me how we are all unique with special talents that we may have to work a bit to see. I hope you can think about that next time you are walking down the hall and looking at all these different kids here in middle school.

"Wow, Your Hair Looks CRAZY Today!"

I remember knowing throughout elementary school, middle school, high school, and even college, that there was something different about me. I knew there was something about the way I looked that was different from the people around me. In middle school, I was very different from my peers. I grew up near Los Angeles, California and I went to a small elementary school and then transferred to a middle school for the seventh grade. This suburb I grew up in was not a diverse place. Do you know what I mean when I say that? The majority of the people who lived there were white, middle- to upper middle-class people. I did not look like my peers. My best friends were blond, blue-eyed girls with fair skin. I was always self-conscious about how both my skin color and hair were darker than everyone else in middle school. I was not a very confident kid in middle school, and I remember just wanting to blend in with everyone else, but that was difficult because I looked so different.

I remember one particular day, it wasn't sunny like it always seems to be in California. It was raining, and somewhat cold. I remember listening to the raindrops against the roof of my classroom. I also remember walking outside in the rain during the passing period. Unfortunately, the rain got my hair really wet and then started trickling down my yellow sweater and I ended up feeling really uncomfortable. Worse yet, when the rain got my hair wet, it grew ten sizes bigger, which it does when it gets wet. The frizz began to reach out and cling to my neighbors. People started looking at me, and saying, "Wow, you look so exotic!" and "Wow, you have cool hair!" or even "Wow, your hair looks CRAZY today!" They may have been trying to be nice, but I really didn't like feeling singled out as different. I felt more alone and different than I had ever felt before. I longed to have straight, blond hair like my friends. I longed to be fair-skinned and not have to worry about the rain and how it made my hair look crazy. They seemed to always look perfect. They all fit in. My friends blended in and I did not. That felt awful.

From that wet day forward, I began to straighten my hair every single day. And you know what? I regret doing that. I wish I had felt that it was okay to be unique, like I do now. I no longer wish I had blond hair and I am really proud of my heritage as a person-of-color. Why do you think I am telling you this story? I'm telling you because I realized that it is okay to be unique and different. But I also know that sometimes, being unique can feel scary, and it can make you feel alone. I hope we can talk about the courage it takes to be our authentic selves.

"I Felt the Earth Might Explode!"

This is a story about how I was different from other kids. When I was really young, I had a lot of anxiety about things. You might have heard of Obsessive Compulsive Disorder or OCD. Sometimes, OCD is thrown around as a joke, but I am a person who really has struggled with some very real aspects of OCD. If you don't know, OCD is when we have intrusive thoughts or feelings that tell us we need to do things a certain way or something bad will happen. For example, when I was young, if I didn't get ready for bed by doing things in a certain order, I felt the earth might explode.

I can remember one day when I was in fifth or sixth grade. I felt the need to do one of my behaviors while I was in class. It was this silly thing where I had to hold my hands pointing in a certain direction for a certain amount of breaths. I remember a classmate noticing this and asking what I was doing. I was lucky in that he wasn't mean to me after I told him, but I was embarrassed and felt very strongly how different I was from everyone else.

I was also really sensitive as a child, which sometimes was seen as a weakness. But I learned over the years it was actually a strength because it helped me know myself and other people really well. I am really good at sensing the world around me and in particular the feelings of other people, which makes me a great therapist. I now know that the anxiety I felt and the worries I had as a young person, were actually a reflection of how strongly I cared about things, which is a good thing. Over the years, my anxiety and OCD have continued to visit me in different ways at different times, but I think about it a lot differently: almost like an annoying, but wise friend that has important messages for me. I'm telling you this story because I think it is important to make friends with the parts of us that make us unique and special and see what we can learn from them, what special gifts they may bring us.

"I Had Never Heard of 'Pride.'"

I remember that in middle school, everyone was starting to talk about dating and romance a lot more than they had previously. Me and my friends spent a lot of time in sixth grade talking about boys, talking about who was cute and who we all liked and didn't like. I remember one night, I had a sleepover with three of my best friends. We were all up late talking about all the people we had a crush on, like we had many times before. As they were all running through their lists, I was thinking about my list and suddenly realized something was very different about me: Their lists were all boys and my list was both boys and girls. I was confused and a little worried about why I was feeling something so different from the people around me. I kept that part of my list to myself for the rest of my middle school experience. I kept dating and I kept talking to people about my crushes, but only ever the boy ones. Having feelings for girls was my secret to keep and I didn't want anyone to know about it.

Fast forward to eighth grade, two years later, and I got an invitation from the local high school to audition for the high school production of the Wizard of Oz™. My sister convinced me to do it by telling me I could hang out with all of her high school friends and meet the people I'd be going to school with next year. I went to the auditions and got a part! I walked into the theatre on the first day of rehearsals to a group of the loudest people I had ever met. They were hollering and yelling and as I got closer I heard they were talking about the "pride parade" coming up. I had never heard of "pride," so I quickly asked them to explain it to me. They told me it was a parade celebrating the queer community, a parade celebrating people who were LGBTQIA+. The group introduced themselves, and from their introductions, I learned that many of them were gay, lesbian, or, like me, bisexual. In that moment I realized I had finally found a group of people who I could tell my secret too. A weight lifted off my shoulders as soon as I spoke my truth, and this thing that had made me feel so sad and different for so long instantly gave me a sense of belonging and community.

Throughout high school, more and more of my friends from middle school came out as queer and were met with acceptance and community. I'm telling you this story, because I think we all have things about us that make us unique and different, things that we might be afraid to share, but sometimes those things that are the scariest and the most unique, are the things that are going to bring us the strongest relationships and community. I wish more than anything that I would have been honest about who I was early, and I know all of my friends feel the same. If we had spoken up about what made us unique, we could have found support and community a lot sooner.

"The Other Part of Me Is Turkish."

Today, I will be telling you a story that involves both my cultural background and my middle-school days. I have a difficult time explaining my culture to people. I was born in America, so part of me feels that the American culture is what I have been surrounded by and with which I mostly identify. The other part of me is Turkish. My parents were both born in Turkey and came to America when they were teenagers. I want to tell you guys a story about the cultural tension I felt growing up.

In eighth grade, I became friends with a new group of kids. These kids were more popular than the other groups of friends I have had in the past. They would wear skinny jeans, wear Vans™, and brand-name clothing. The group also consisted of boys and girls, which was considered "cooler" back in my middle school. I also thought one of the boys might have a little crush on me. I noticed that the parents of these kids were very chill and laid back. These kids could hang out whenever they wanted and the girls in the group had sleepovers all the time. I really wanted to be part of this group so I tried to do as much as I could with them.

I remember one specific day very vividly. My new friends and I had planned to go to the movies to see Iron Man™ (the first one). It was a cold but sunny spring day. We had been talking about seeing this movie for a few weeks. I didn't care so much about the movie, but I wanted to go with my group of friends. I had begged my dad to let me go to the movies and he finally said yes.

The day of the movie came and all my friends' parents dropped them off at the movies. I remember my dad telling me that he was going to pick me up in front of the movie theater immediately after the movie was over. I remember having a great time at the movies and while walking out of the theater, my friends came up with an idea: Target™ was right down the street and they all decided they wanted to walk there after the movie and hang out. However, I looked outside and saw that my dad was already waiting for me. My friends' parents didn't mind them walking and being out on their own, but I knew my family cared about that. I remember walking out with my group of friends and asking my dad if I could walk with them to Target™ and have him pick me up later. My dad said no. I got pretty mad and kept asking him, saying I was going to stay with them. My dad started speaking and yelling at me to get in the car in Turkish. That is my family's native language and the first language I ever learned.

I remember turning red and feeling so embarrassed. I used to hate when my parents spoke to me in anything but English. I ran inside the movie theater and my dad drove off. I ended up going with my friends to Target™ and then getting a ride back home with my friend's mom. I still remember that day and the embarrassment I felt.

I am telling you this story because I wanted to be vulnerable and share something unique about myself and my upbringing. My culture is very family oriented. A lot of things are done with the family and the family is highly respected and loved. I regret getting so mad at my dad and not being able to embrace my unique cultural and familial differences back in eighth grade. I wish I would have realized that my dad was trying to keep me safe and that speaking another language is actually pretty cool. Now, I embrace and love my uniqueness and I hope you can too.

"It Is Okay to Be Different."

When I was in fourth grade, my teacher told my parents she thought I might have some learning challenges. I always felt behind in class, and I had a hard time paying attention and following the teacher's instructions. My parents took me to see the School Psychologist and she gave me a bunch of tests. I ended up getting diagnosed with ADHD (which made it a challenge for me to focus my attention) and Dyslexia (which made it hard for me to read and write).

At first, these diagnoses made me feel really different than other kids, especially when I would have to go to the nurse's office during recess to get my medication, or when my learning plan with my teachers gave me special accommodations during certain activities that no one else had (I could take more time for tests, for example). When I got to middle school, I still felt different than my friends and people in my grade. To make it worse, I went to a small middle school with the same kids from my elementary school. All of the people in my grade knew I had "learning disabilities." Even their parents knew! I felt really self-conscious about the things that I struggled with. I started to have low self-esteem, especially when it seemed like things that I had a hard time doing were really easy for other kids, like turning in my homework on time, finding my calculator, or reading out loud in class.

I was often self-conscious that somebody would tease me or make fun of me for my learning disabilities, so I learned to make jokes about myself first, especially with my close friends. Sometimes I'd play up the things I was bad at and then joke about them. I felt like if I made fun of myself first, then other people wouldn't have a chance to. But inside, I was ashamed of my diagnoses, and I felt like I wasn't as good as the other people in my class.

One night at a sleepover party with three of my best friends, I was really hyper and was bouncing on my friend's bed and knocked over a glass of juice. My friend April was annoyed about the juice and looked at me and said "Oh my god Malia, it's like you're too ADHD to function." My other friends laughed at what she said, and I felt my whole body turning red because I felt so embarrassed. My mind kind of froze and I didn't know what to say. April had just revealed my biggest insecurity. I had been joking and putting my own self down about it for so long, but I felt so sad and lonely at that moment that I went to the bathroom and cried.

If I could go back now and talk to my younger self then, I would tell young Malia a few things: I would say first that it is okay to be different. In fact, it's a pretty great thing to have a brain that's wired a little bit differently than the people around you. It means you think outside of the box. It also means that you have to practice working hard at things that challenge you, so when big challenges happen in life, you're even more equipped to handle them. I wish I could have told my younger self that having ADHD doesn't just mean that you aren't as good at certain things, but it also means that you have extra strengths in other areas that other people don't always have. I wish back then I could have been proud of my differences instead of trying to hide them or put myself down before other people could. And I hope we can talk about how each of you can be proud of your differences too, about what makes you unique.

"She Was Making Us Caldo."

I am going to tell you all a story about when I was in middle school. This story is very difficult to tell because it involves a time where I was being bullied for being different. Even though I am an adult it is very hard for me to share a personal story with you all. So, thanks in advance for being respectful while I tell my story.

When I was in middle school I started hanging out with a group of girls. We didn't really have much in common, but I thought they were so cool. I thought that by hanging out with them I would also be cool. We would hang out with each other during school but rarely hung out after school. My parents had just bought me and my siblings a trampoline and I was so excited. I thought it would be a great idea to invite my friends over to my house to play. I begged my mom to let me have my friends over, she normally didn't let me have friends at our house. After begging for days, my parents finally agreed, so I went to school and invited my friends to my house after school on Friday.

I was so excited all day: I couldn't wait to show my friends my room and hopefully we could find more common interests. I went home that afternoon and cleaned my room and put on some "cool" clothes because we had to wear uniforms to school. My friends knocked on the door and I let them in, and the first thing they said was: "Oh my god! What's that smell?" I was so confused I didn't smell anything, as we moved further into my house, they kept making comments, making fake gagging noises, and laughing. We finally got to the kitchen and my mom was making us dinner. She was making us "Caldo" which is a Mexican hot stew made with beef and vegetables. My mom asked if they wanted any and one responded by saying, "Eww, no, that looks gross." Another responded with, "No, it doesn't look very good." They stayed at my house for a while, but they left early. I was so embarrassed I didn't eat dinner that night. I cried in my room because I was so ashamed.

The next day during lunch I went to hang out with my friends, and I heard them telling other people how much my house smelled and how it was gross. They did not hang out with me anymore and I was so sad. Other people in my class made comments to me saying that I ate stinky food. I didn't invite anyone to my house again for the whole year. I tried not to eat my family's food and asked for hotdogs and hamburgers. I didn't want to speak Spanish in public anymore, I was so ashamed of who I was. It wasn't until my seventh grade year I started hanging out with other Latina girls and I talked to them about this situation. They told me that Caldo was their favorite food: I was so shocked! We talked more and I found out we had so many things in common and their families ate similar foods to my family.

I'm telling you this story because I want you all to remember to embrace what makes you unique, which is sometimes your culture. I hope you can enjoy your own culture's food because the people who made fun of me in middle school are now posting on Instagram asking for authentic Mexican restaurant recommendations! I am also telling you this story so that you are aware of other's differences, and how culture can be something that makes us unique. Unlike the girls in my story, we all need to be respectful and sensitive to those differences. The world would be so boring if we didn't get to share our culture, enjoy other cultures, and share what makes us unique. Thank you all for listening and allowing me to share a very sad moment in my middle school experience.

"She Wanted Hair Like Mine?"

From elementary school through most of high school, there was one thing about me I was pretty embarrassed by – my hair. Obviously, as you can see, I have big, thick, curly red hair. While some people have told me they thought it was pretty, for a really long time I thought it was frizzy, ratty, coarse, too big and not how I wanted to get attention. I can remember kids in my middle school hallway calling me "Miss Frizzle" (the teacher from The Magic School Bus™). I always pretended I didn't hear, but every time someone made fun of my hair, I remembered it. Whenever I did get a compliment (usually from an adult), it didn't matter because I always remembered what the kids at school would say. I would rather have gotten a compliment on my personality or style than my hair because I never felt like my hair was my choice.

But it wasn't just my hair, I felt awkward about my appearance generally – my nose, my freckles, my lanky legs. I wanted to be beautiful like Aisha Compton – she was blonde, tan, and popular. All the kids liked her and she always had on the coolest clothes and makeup. I remember trying to dress and do my makeup like Aisha did for a long time. I'd wear lots of eyeliner and put clips in my hair. I also always wore my hair up because I felt like wearing it down would be asking for too much attention.

One day in seventh grade, I accidentally overslept and had to race to school. I didn't have time to put on the makeup and hair clips like I normally did. I remember feeling so worried I would look bad without my "pretty girl costume." I had gym class that day and when I was at my locker, I noticed the girl next to me whom I hadn't talked to much. Her name was Helen, and she looked at me and said, "Normally you wear so much eyeliner, but you're not today. I think it looks good. You have really pretty eyes. Also, I like your hair." I was shocked because I was sure she was going to make fun of me. I said, "Thank you, sometimes I think it's embarrassing." She said, "I think it's cool. I wish I had cool hair like you instead of boring straight hair like mine." She wanted hair like mine? I couldn't believe it because all I wanted was straight, shiny hair: The kind I could run my finger through and flip around. She wanted what I had!

I always remembered what Helen said. It took me a really long time to get comfortable with my hair, I would straighten it or only wear it up, but now I love it and realize it's part of who I am. It's also not the only unique thing about me. As I got older, I discovered things people couldn't see that make me unique, like my interests and my feelings. I'm telling you this because I want you to know that I understand what it's like to not always be happy about what makes you unique. I also want you to listen to the cheerleaders in your life who highlight and celebrate your uniqueness. Helen was the first of many people who complimented my hair and helped me accept it. There will always be critics, but there will also always be kind people who want to lift you up.

"I Didn't Have Much of a Choice in How I Looked."

I'm going to tell a story about being unique, are we all ready to listen and support? Growing up, my family was very different from most of the other families in our town. I am the oldest of eight kids, and my parents were very religious and had a lot of strict rules that other families didn't have. My brothers and sisters and I were homeschooled, which means we didn't go to the public school like everyone else, so we were home almost all of the time. I wasn't allowed to go do many things outside my house, like sports or clubs, and I didn't have many friends, because most of the time I was expected to be home helping with chores and taking care of the younger kids.

My family was a group I belonged to, but in that group, there wasn't really any room for being unique. In order to belong I had to be like everyone else. I was unique and different from the other people in my town, because my family was different, but that felt less like being special and more like just being a weirdo. People would stare at us when we were in public or driving because there were just so many of us. I was pretty good at staying in my role in my family and not trying to be my own different person, because belonging in the family was very important to me. The times I did try to be myself a little bit, it didn't go that well.

When I was about 13, I had a job that I would go to once a week. Somebody we knew owned a pharmacy, and I would go help them keep the shelves clean and put on price tags and things like that. Because of that job, I had a little bit of money that was my own. One thing about my family is that we were poor, so my parents didn't have money to spend on clothes for us kids. Almost all of our clothes were hand-me-downs, which means they were clothes that other people had worn and didn't want anymore: Basically, I just wore whatever people gave us that fit me. I didn't have much of a choice in how I looked.

One day, I asked my mom to take me to a store to get some new jeans with my money from my job. It wasn't a fancy store, and they weren't "name brand" jeans or anything. I just wanted some jeans that were dark wash and weren't worn out in the knees. She took me to the story and I spent my own money: I think it was $10 or $20 each for two pairs of brand-new jeans. One dark blue and one black. I was so excited, because they looked so fresh and new and dark.

When we got home, I showed my dad my new jeans because I was excited. He was not excited: He got upset that I had spent so much money on new jeans, instead of getting them used. I was so surprised and frustrated, because I had spent my own money, not his. I thought I should be able to do what I wanted with my own money. He was going to make me take both pairs back, but my mom helped argue my case, and he decided I could keep one pair. He thought it was important that I learn about going to thrift stores and getting a good bargain, so he took me to the thrift store the next day. He was excited because we found three pairs of jeans that fit me for 25 cents each. He was trying to teach me about good money management, but I hated those jeans because I didn't like the way they fit. I didn't feel good in them, and they were all light and worn out looking. They just weren't the ones I had wanted.

Because of the way my family worked, with no room for me to be unique, I have spent a lot of my adult life trying to figure out how to be my own person. I still get stressed out sometimes trying to buy clothes, or making other choices, because it's hard for me to figure out what I like. I didn't get much practice until after I moved out of my parent's house.

I'm telling you this story because it can sometimes be tricky to figure out how to be unique and be yourself while belonging to a group. Sometimes families or friend groups don't make room for each person to be unique, and the only way to belong to that group is to try to be like everyone else. But sometimes there are groups or families that create a safe enough space for each person to be unique while still belonging. I want you to know that the belonging/being unique balance is something that people are managing for their entire lives, even as adults. It's something I'm still learning. When you can find places to be your own unique self, while also belonging, that is a very special thing.

Index

For Product Safety Concerns and Information please contact our EU
representative GPSR@taylorandfrancis.com
Taylor & Francis Verlag GmbH, Kaufingerstraße 24, 80331 München, Germany

9 781032 437675